Ministrycraft

Ministrycraft

A very personal look at some
aspects of the "craft" of ministry

John C Nicol

Spiderwize

Ministrycraft

Spiderwize
Mews Cottage
The Causeway, Kennoway
Kingdom of Fife
KY8 5JU
Scotland UK

www.spiderwize.com

ISBN: 978-1-907294-18-1

To the people who have helped to turn "Ministrycraft" from a vague dream into reality – Anne Nicol, Maria Shaw, Sandra Boyd and Ron Blakey

Contents

Introduction

What's this book about, who's it for and what's the plan?

There is no doubt that a sense of vocation is essential for anyone wanting to be involved in ministry. No one in their right senses would do it for the money, the hours are long, the demands are great, and there can be lots of disappointment and frustrations. That is why ministry is only for those who have a sense of being "called" to it. But that sense of call is only the beginning - what we need after that is to acquire a wide variety of skills and abilities either through learning or through experience. I like to think of that ongoing process as the "craft" of ministry or "ministrycraft". The word "craft" suggests that a person has skills and experience in a particular area, and implies that it is very much a "hands on" experience. For example a diplomat may be described as being skilled in "statecraft" and that assumes not just theoretical knowledge but working experience and proven ability in all the different aspects of government, politics, and international affairs. You have walked the corridors of power and have survived! If your abilities lie in "woodcraft" that does not just mean that you are good at carving objects in wood, but that you are essentially a country person, at home on the moor and in the forest, recognising birds and animals and plants, and reading the signs that nature leaves for those who understand them. It may be that your particular craft is "witchcraft" and leaving aside whether that is or is not a good thing, it suggests that you do not just know the theory but the practice as well - that you can conjure up a spell or two at the drop of a broomstick!

This book is about how I see the "craft" of ministry or "ministrycraft." It is a very personal view of some of the different skills and abilities and understandings which I believe go to make up ministry today. It is gleaned from twenty seven years of service as a Church of Scotland minister both overseas and at home and ten years working in the administration of the NHS, as well as seven years of study at Glasgow University and in the USA and three years of evening study to obtain a qualification in NHS administration.

Like any craft there will be some people who have a natural aptitude for one particular aspect of "ministrycraft" just as there are those who take naturally to one aspect of statecraft or woodcraft. But at the same time much if not all of the craft of ministry can be learned and that learning happens in a wide variety of ways - from lectures, study and books as students; from the "hands-on" experience and practice of ministry; from ongoing personal reflection and reading while in-service; and from sharing with others and learning from others through courses, conferences, support groups and fraternals. It is my hope that this book can make a small contribution to the learning and development of your "ministrycraft." I make no claim that it covers all aspects of ministry for no doubt I have sub-consciously and even consciously tended to focus on the aspects which are of special interest to me. If it speaks to you, inspires you a little, or even irritates you into action on any aspect of "ministrycraft" I shall be more than content.

If you are looking for a treatise on the theological background to the nature of Christian ministry this book is not for you! If you are searching for profound insights into the nature of the vocation of ministry it is not for you either! But if you are in the enquiry phase or you are a candidate preparing for ministry, I hope that it may give you some pointers about actually doing the job. If you are in the early years of your first charge it might help with some of those practical issues no one told you you would be facing. If you are a church member involved in or thinking of volunteering to help in some aspect of ministry such as worship or pastoral care (or being thrust into service by your enthusiastic pastor!) or even serving on a Nomination Committee I hope that it can help you. If you are feeling that perhaps God may be calling you to ministry but are not ready to talk to anyone face to face, you can perhaps get some idea from these pages of what ministry is all about. If you are a serving minister, auxiliary, deacon or reader, interested in discovering how someone else tackles some of the basic tasks of ministry, you may find it of interest. Inevitably I bring to it my background as a Church of Scotland minister, though I hope that much of what I say will be relevant to those who minister in all denominations of the Christian Church. If it all seems too common sense and obvious I shall regard that as a compliment rather than a criticism.

The plan is straight-forward – to look in some detail at what I consider to be the two most important aspects of ministrycraft – worship and pastoral care, and then to explore various other aspects which have emerged in my experience as significant (some of which may at times be neglected) including communication, styles of ministry, sharing ministry, the management side of ministry, being a good employer, using time well, and coping with stress. To keep things simple I have assumed a church management structure with one body in charge which I have called the Kirk Session following the new Unitary Constitution introduced by the General Assembly of the Church of Scotland in 2003. If your denomination or congregation is different from this please adjust your set accordingly!

John C Nicol

Chapter 1

Crafting Worship – Time, Language and Resources

When I retired we moved into a brand new house and because of this I had to face a range of DIY challenges for the first time for many years! The only table we could find that was the right size and shape for the entrance hall came from Ikea and was still in its natural state. I assured my wife that it would be easy to stain and polish it and reached for my DIY manual. My first thought was French polishing, but when I read about all the different stages required, the variety of processes involved, and the attention to detail needed, I opted instead for a packet of sandpaper and a tin of pine varnish from B & Q!

It seems natural to begin our look at ministrycraft with worship. To say that it is central to what we do as ministers is to state the obvious. What is equally obvious to all of us who are involved in worship is that this is the French polishing of "ministrycraft." It requires different stages and involves a variety of processes. It takes time, patience and skill. It is neither simple nor easy, and if we are going to do it well we have to be ready to give it our full attention and every bit of our ability. I want to look at eight different aspects of worship in turn and we shall do that in the chapters that follow -

Theming, Praising, Praying, Preaching, Sharing and Enabling, Breaking the Mould, Children versus Adults and Celebrating.

But first of all let us look at three topics that are important in all aspects of worship - Time, Language and Resources.

Time

What really put me off the French polishing was the amount of time it was going to take. Crafting worship takes time! There is no way around that, and if we are serious about producing the best from our crafting with all the tools we have at our disposal, then we have to make sure that we allocate sufficient time to it. We are going to talk about the whole question of time management in chapter 22 but we need to say at this stage what everyone agrees in theory but does not always follow in practice - that our very first priority in organising our weekly working timetable should be time for the preparation of worship. For all of us who are involved in ministry this is the most important thing we do - expressing our faith in worship and seeking to help other people to express their faith in worship. Because of that it is not simply a question of finding time when we are free from other commitments. Time for worship preparation needs to be quality time, when we are bright- eyed and bushy-tailed, the house is quiet and our minds are focused; not when we get home from a funeral, the kids are running riot, the TV is blaring, or we are preoccupied about how to deal with a tricky situation in the Kirk Session later in the evening. Naturally the actual time we choose is up to us, because we all have different life styles and function in different ways. I found that the best way for me was to simply mark off the whole of every Thursday for worship preparation. That usually meant that by evening meal time on Thursday I was well on my way, and that I could then decide either to bash on into the evening in order to have the satisfaction of knowing it was complete, or leave it until Friday morning. If you find yourself instinctively responding to that with words like "Lucky thing!" or "Smarty Pants!" or "All very well for him, I could never do that!" then stop and ask yourself what is so different or exceptional about your situation that makes this kind of prioritising of worship impossible. Over the years I found that as the members of the congregation came to accept that Thursday was "sermon day" it not only gave me the necessary space, but gave them an insight into the importance of preparation for worship and by implication of worship itself. As I listen to fellow ministers talking about their busy schedules I become increasingly concerned that preparation for worship may lose its first priority in favour of a multiplicity of tasks and roles which make up ministry today. There will always be "the week from hell" when we find that we finally sit down to think about the sermon on Saturday at 6 pm, but if that happens with any regularity we really need to stop and ask ourselves whether this is good - for ourselves, our family, our congregation, or our God!

Language

Words are the raw material of worship. Of course there are other things that are important, like music and silence, but most of what we do in worship relies on words. So that makes the words we choose to use very important and the way in which we put them together absolutely crucial. And that brings us face to face with a very big decision which everyone involved in worship has to make. On the one hand we can decide that worship is such a unique and special event that we should use special words in a special way to emphasise that uniqueness, echoing by and large the unique language of the King James version of the Bible. Or we can decide that worship needs to be part of our living and our everyday experience and use words that are as far as possible normal and contemporary. To give just one example of this distinction, this is part of the opening prayer for the Sacrament of Holy Communion in the 1940 Book of Common Order of the Church of Scotland :

"Eternal God our heavenly Father, who admittest thy people into such wonderful Communion that, partaking by a divine mystery of the body and blood of Thy dear Son, they should dwell in Him and He in them; we unworthy sinners, approaching thy presence and beholding Thy glory, do repent us of our transgressions."

By way of contrast this is part of the same prayer from the 1994 version of Common Order :

"Most merciful God,
we confess that we have sinned,
in thought word and deed,
through our own fault
and in common with others.
We are truly sorry
and turn humbly from our sins."

In practice most of us do not make such an absolute choice one way or the other in the words that we use and how we use them in worship and probably most of us try to use language that is familiar and everyday though stopping short of the extremes of informality and slang.

One of the turning points in my worshipcraft came in 1967 when I was serving with the Church of Scotland in Buenos Aires, Argentina, under the quaintly entitled "Colonial and Continental Committee." After reading a review in Life and Work I ordered and received a copy of Contemporary Prayers for Public Worship, a collection of prayers from a group of Congregationalist ministers, edited by Caryl Micklem and published by SCM Press. Maybe this book did not quite change my life, but it certainly changed my worship, and the language of my worship! For the first time I realised fully that since I was confident God would understand anyway whatever language I used, the most important thing was to use language and thought forms that would be meaningful and easily understood to those whom I was seeking to lead in worship. I wore that book out, so much so that in 1988 I had to have it rebound! It is no longer in print in the original, but an updated version was published in 1993 - Contemporary Prayers - The Collected Edition. Here is part of a Communion Prayer from that book:

> "Lord Jesus, once more in the midst of a busy life we gather to ask for bread - strength to continue the journey, inspiration to call your kingdom into being about us as we go. We bring ordinary bread, but you make it special bread by sharing your life with us as we break it together. Help us also to carry the special into the ordinary. Let your presence among us give point to everything we do."

The Congregationalists were not alone in this trend, and the introduction to Contemporary Prayers for Public Worship mentions William Barclay, George MacLeod and Michel Quoist as being in the vanguard of the movement towards the use of familiar language. Another more quirky approach came before that from a Methodist, David Head, whose three little books – He Sent Leanness, Stammerer's Tongue and Shout For Joy published in 1959 1960 and 1961 broke new ground with their delightful humour and natural language but also incisive meaning. Here is a small sample :

> "We pray that our statesmen may do everything they can to promote peace, so long as our own national history and honour and pride and prosperity and superiority and sovereignty are maintained.
>
> *You can do all things, O God."*

Since then much has happened and there is a wealth of material, all of which encourages us as leaders of worship to use not just contemporary language but contemporary ideas in our worship.

We in the Church of Scotland are fortunate in that our tradition gives us the freedom to use our own words throughout services of worship. Those denominations with fixed liturgies face a bigger challenge if they wish to use language and ideas that are current and relevant. Having shared in worship on Palm Sunday and Easter Day recently with a congregation using an Anglican liturgy for Communion I realise with concern that there is a widening gulf between denominations in the kind of language being used in worship.

Just in case we think that "contemporary" and "relevant" means dull and unpoetic, here is the opening of a prayer by George MacLeod entitled "The Cost of A Changing Day":

Ever present God:
Everything is in your hands.
You ordained everything.
You made all ages a preparation for the coming of your Son.
You called your people out of Egypt to cradle Him.
Your prophets foretold Him, son of David, infant of Mary.
And when the time was ripe He came:
Wielding the hammer,
treading the winepress,
tramping the earth,
contradicting the smooth,
giving hope to the sinners,
redeeming the world.
Ever present God:
Everything is still in Your hands.
Out of eternity You have called each one of us
Into Your Church.

Resources

There is a curious kind of reverse snobbery among some worship leaders in the Church of Scotland and other denominations with a "free" liturgy which says that unless you write it yourself or compose it yourself in the pulpit it is not any good. That is to ignore the huge wealth of resources that are available to us as part of the Christian Church. But more than that it can mean that our worship can become very self-focused and narrow. Of course making use of resources does not usually mean using whole prayers or sermons out of books, and one of the ways in which resource material can help us is in sparking ideas, expanding horizons and exploring new directions. I am not ashamed to admit that I have often found myself stuck for a new way of approaching the opening prayers of Adoration and Confession, only to pick up a book and find the seed of word or idea that got me going.

In the field of resources, there is an embarrassment of riches for us to delve into. Naturally every denomination has its equivalent of the Church of Scotland's Common Order and it can be illuminating to study those with which we are less familiar. I suspect I am not alone in finding it difficult Sunday after Sunday to make the prayer of Dedication of the Offering relevant to the theme, but at the same time express the dedication of the people to God as well as the offering, while keeping it all short and snappy. So I am always on the lookout for new inspiration and just to give one example on a recent visit to the USA picked up "When We Gather - A Book of Prayers for Worship" by James G Kirk (Presbyterian USA). It is worth remembering that people have been leading worship for a very long time and delving back into material from past centuries (eg The Book of Psalms!) can be surprisingly stimulating. Recognising also that a sense of worship and spirituality crosses many boundaries and that prayers and meditations from other world religions can give us inspiration can open us up to many fresh insights. The Oxford Book of Prayer has an excellent section - Prayers from Other Traditions of Faith.

It is impossible to list here all the possible sources of material for worship we can tap into so I shall content myself with mentioning three -

1 Iona Abbey Worship Book and others from Wild Goose Publications (www.ionabooks.com)

2 Publications related to Churches Together in Britain and Ireland (www.ctbi.org.uk)

3 Starters for Sunday – suggested readings, prayers, hymns and songs for Sunday worship from the Church of Scotland (www.churchofscotland.org.uk/worship)

You can find directions to a much fuller list of books about worship and worship resources in Appendix A.

But beyond books and publications specifically relating to worship, there is a sense in which everything you read can help with your crafting of worship, because everything you read feeds your mind and your spirit with words and ideas. If you run out of books you can always turn to the Internet and I defy anyone to exhaust the resources there. But as we all know quantity does not always mean quality and you can spend a lot of time looking for something helpful. Experience has shown that if you have to pay for it, there is a better chance of it being useful and on this basis I have paid a small annual subscription for a number of years to gain access to a USA website which offers a wide variety of worship material including sermons, illustrations, worship aids, children's talks, dramas and powerpoint presentations with flexible charging rates. (www.esermons.com) Another USA site which offers masses of links to other sites is Jenee Woodward's "The Text This Week - Lectionary, Scripture Study and Worship Links and Resources" (www.textweek.com). One good Scottish site is www.multimedia.its forministry.org which has a variety of materials developed by Donald McCorkindale. Naturally a lot of background resources overlap between worship and preaching and we shall return to this topic in chapter 5.

Undoubtedly the best resource I have found in crafting worship including sermons over the last twenty years has been the discipline of regular daily bible study using bible study notes. My own particular favourite is "Guidelines" published by The Bible Reading Fellowship but of course there are many others and you will find one that suits you personally. I have absolutely no doubt that the value of daily bible study is immense, even if it is only ten or fifteen minutes every day, simply because it is every day and over the years that builds up almost without us noticing. Nor is it only helpful in increasing our overall knowledge of the Bible though of course it does that - it can give often give us ideas for specific sermons and for that reason is it always worth doing your daily study with a pen and some blank cards at your side, so that if something occurs to you you can immediately jot down the details with a reference to your Bible Study Notes so that you can trace it later.

Having thought about these general questions of Time, Language and Resources we are now ready to look at each of the different aspects of worship in turn.

Chapter 2

Crafting Worship – Theming

One of the most difficult things about preparing worship is making a start! I know this from my own experience and from that of probationers whom I have worked with and members of congregations who have become involved. There is nothing more frightening than a blank expanse of A4 writing pad or printer paper when the deadline of Sunday morning at 11 am is looming! Somehow once there is something down on paper that makes things better, and that is probably why we are all tempted to rush into pen or print as quickly as possible. But the danger is that if we simply start off writing a prayer or perhaps a Children's Address, there is no consistency in what we are doing, and we finish up with a Service made up of isolated items which may be good in themselves, but have no link to each other. This is particularly noticeable in the kind of Sunday morning worship that is common in the Church of Scotland where the Children's Address may be an injunction to the children to be good like Jesus, while the sermon invites the adults to accept God's forgiveness for their failure to be good like Jesus! At its worst the lack of any kind of theme in a Service means that the prayers, praise and sermon have nothing to do with each other and the congregation is left confused and uncertain about what to take home with them in the way of a message.

Finding a theme for a Service is not as difficult as it sounds. On most occasions it will arise naturally out of the text or passage chosen for the sermon, and means simply that the items of praise chosen and the content of the prayers should echo and reinforce that theme. But it does suggest that the first task in preparation for worship is the sermon, and that only once that is completed or well under way, can the other parts of the Service be woven around it. It may be also that a theme will present itself for the whole Service, particularly on Christian festivals like Christmas and Easter or special occasions like Harvest Thanksgiving or Admission of New Members. Nor does the theme need to be immovable and rigid. On the contrary it can develop and grow through the Service and in the Children's Address, and prayers as well as the sermon itself. Some of the best sermons that I have heard preached have effectively begun in the Children's Address and ended in the Prayers of Thanksgiving and Intercession.

Almost as scary as a blank sheet of paper, is moving into a new house and having to decide what to do with each room in the way of furnishings and decoration. We have all watched enough "make-over" programmes on TV to know that the answer is always to have some idea of an overall theme for each room both in colour and in style. We all know how pleasing it is when it works well - the curtains complement the carpets, and contrast beautifully with the wall coverings. Our crafting of worship makes similar demands of us, that we keep in the forefront of our thinking and preparing an overall idea of what the theme is, so that the result is a whole woven together into a unity.

Theming matters - not just for the satisfaction of a job well done for those who prepare worship, but for those who have come to share in worship. The more we are able to weave together each part of the Service, the easier it will be for those who are in the pews to grasp the message we want to convey to them, and the greater will be their sense of participation in something that has shape and purpose.

A simple example will help to clarify what I am talking about. We might want to construct a service around the words of Jesus in John 8 : 12 "I am the light of the world" and in Matthew 5 : 13 "You are like light for the whole world." The theme of Jesus as the light of the world could be introduced in the talk to the children where we could explore with them different kinds of light – candles, torches, electric bulbs, laser etc – interpreting how the love of Jesus shines out in our world. Prayers of Adoration could acknowledge the importance of light in the created world while prayers of confession could admit that we need the forgiveness of God to move from the darkness of sin into his light. The sermon might lead on from reassurance – Jesus is the light of the world and our light – to challenge – we are called by him to be light to the world. Prayers of thanksgiving and intercession could give concrete examples of situations where the light is shining and where the light needs to shine brighter. It would not be difficult to find suitable hymns and songs to suit this theme – "Shine Jesus, shine" "Christ be our light" "Christ is our light! The bright and morning star" "Christ is the world's true light" "I the Lord of sea and sky" and "As a fire is meant for burning" would fit well into the theme.

Chapter 3

Crafting Worship – Praising

"I didn't know any of these hymns this morning!" That is probably something that sooner or later will be said to you - it certainly has been said to me. But before we start feeling too sorry for ourselves, it is worth realising that such comments reflect a very important fact - that people relate to the praise in worship more than to anything else. "At least we had a good sing" is just another way of making it clear that the hymns and songs we choose for worship are crucial in creating a link between the worship we prepare and those who share in it. It is outside the scope of this book to examine the centuries-long story of the place of praise and music in worship - suffice to say that singing seems to have been a vital part of worship from the earliest days of the church just as it is today. It is because the praise really matters to people today that we have to bring all our crafting skills and abilities to the vital task of choosing the right songs and hymns to sing in worship.

So what are the issues in choosing praise?

Relevance

In the light of what I have said already about Theming, it goes without saying that we should whenever possible try to choose items of praise that relate to the theme for the Service. In that context it is worth bearing in mind that a hymn or song which really sums up the entire message of the worship is best sung towards the end of the Service, particularly after the sermon has done its bit to explain and develop the theme. Some of the books of praise currently in use give very helpful detailed indexes by theme which make this job easier. Otherwise it is a matter of looking at the contents page at the beginning and trying to determine where we are most likely to find the right hymns. Some of the websites I mentioned on pages 8 and 9 can be helpful, particularly if you like to follow the lectionary. My own experience is that there is no substitute for browsing, and flicking through books of songs and hymns can often produce something surprisingly appropriate. But there will also be times when you can find nothing that relates to your theme, or when you wish to emphasise through praise one aspect of the service of worship. For example it can be helpful to those whom you are leading in worship to follow the prayers of thanksgiving and intercession with a hymn or song of thanksgiving. That is another way of adding to worship by choosing praise which is relevant. Beyond that, there may be times when we do not want to be too specific in our quest for relevance but rather make use of an appropriate choice from the many general hymns and songs of worship and praise which are available to us. What is to be avoided if at all possible is including in a service an item of praise which is clearly inappropriate. A harvest hymn on christmas Sunday would be an extreme example, but requests are often made for baptismal hymns at wedding services, and including triumphant Easter hymns during Holy Week is to miss the mood of these special days.

Familiarity

There is nothing more satisfying if you enjoy singing in church than joining in your favourite hymn, psalm or song. One of my own favourites is still Ian Pitt-Watson's version of Psalm 139, "You are before me, God, you are behind" to the tune Sursum Corda which happily made it from CH3 into CH4. If you want to be instantly popular in your congregation, you will choose praise that is well known and well loved and never attempt anything new. The trouble with doing that is that the congregation's repertoire is never enlarged, staleness sets in, and the vast wealth of new and exciting church music remains untapped. On the other hand if the praise in a service of worship consists entirely of unfamiliar items, many of those present will go home less than happy and our efforts to introduce new praise will have had entirely the wrong result. The secret of course is no secret at all - as everyone knows it is to get a good balance between the familiar and the well-loved and the new and innovative. I have always worked on the premise that you can get away with one completely unfamiliar item of praise in a service with say, five hymns and songs. Exactly how to introduce new praise is open to debate - some congregations devote time before worship begins to practising a new item, while others rely on picking up the tune when the organist plays it over - though that only works if the whole tune is played and not a truncated version as seems to be the practice in many churches. If it is not suitable to practice a song before the service, then I think it is a good idea for the person leading worship to announce the song, recognise that it is unfamiliar, and invite the congregation to listen to the tune as it is played over. My own particular hate, is stopping in the middle of the worship to practise the praise that is about to be sung!

Good Words and Music

There are lots of amusing little gems hidden away in the words of our hymn books and song books if you go looking for them.

The Plumbers' Hymn, "O Christ in thee my soul hath found" continues in verse 3 –

> "I tried the broken cisterns Lord,
> But ah! The waters failed."

Well the waters would fail, wouldn't they if the cistern was broken?

Or what about The Dry Cleaners' Hymn –
"Come my soul, thy suit prepare." RCH 450)

Arthritis sufferers might join in singing –
"O lift thou up the sinking hand,
Confirm the feeble knee." (CH3 669)

The Garden Designers favourite may well be –
"Every joy or trial falleth from above,
Traced upon our dial by the sun of love." (Mission Praise 421)

But the prize has to go to the nudist choir and orchestra who were thus encouraged –
"Strings and voices, hands and hearts,
In the concert bear your parts." (CH3 359)

On a more serious note I am puzzled by our apparent need to sing anything and everything whether it suits or not to the tune of "Amazing Grace", most recently the magnificent words of the metrical version of Psalm 23, The Lord's my shepherd. Now the same thing seems to be happening with the ubiquitous "Highland Cathedral."

Both the words and the music matter, and choosing praise simply on the basis of whether the tune is lively, singable, or easily learnt, while totally ignoring the words just will not do. But the opposite extreme is equally undesirable - focusing entirely on meaningful words while avoiding altogether the issue of whether the tune is known, can be learnt, or is too difficult for an average congregation. One tendency which I personally regret is to try to solve the tension of words versus music by starting with the "right" words and then singing them to any tune we can find of the same metre which is known and easy. The original matching of words with music is likely to be something that has involved a great deal of time and effort on the part of composer and editor, and simply plucking another tune out of the hymn book is hardly doing justice to either words or music.

During my time in ministry nothing short of a revolution has taken place. I still have a copy of "Thirty Twentieth Century Hymns" which was first published in 1960 and contained such exciting new items as "Lord Jesus Christ, you have come to us" with both words and music by Patrick Appleford, and the tune Camberwell for "At the name of Jesus" composed by Michael Brierley. Looking back it does appear that the lead in the incredible flowering of new church music that followed came from the Anglican tradition with Galliard in the forefront, but of course in more recent times it has been John Bell and Graham Maule with Wild Goose in Scotland that has been the dominant influence in this direction. One of their unique contributions has been to sympathetically marry traditional scottish airs with good modern words to achieve worship songs that are new, yet rest on a long and unique musical heritage. "Christ's is the world in which we move" to the old scottish melody "Dream Angus" is just one excellent example in which the haunting tune is combined with words that are unforgettable:

> "To the lost Christ shows his face,
> To the unloved he gives his embrace,
> To those who cry in pain or disgrace,
> Christ makes, with his friends, a touching place." (CH4 724)

Today, there is an excess of riches! The difficulty is not in finding good songs and hymns, but in choosing from all that are available. There are many collections of songs and hymns, such as Songs of God's People, Mission Praise, Common Ground, and Songs of Fellowship, and new material is constantly appearing to complement the more traditional hymn books of the major denominations. The Church Hymnary Fourth Edition published in 2005 is a big book at a big price but big too in richness of choice and will repay careful perusal and regular use.   The result of so much material is that churches face a real dilemma if they wish to sing a variety of traditional and modern songs and hymns in worship - which particular selection to purchase for use by the congregation. Given the cost of hard-backed books this is an expensive exercise for even a moderately sized congregation and it is important to examine all the alternatives carefully before making a final choice. Some congregations are solving this problem in a different way by printing the words for the items of praise in a weekly worship leaflet or putting them on a screen and taking out a copyright licence through CCLI (Christian Copyright Licensing International). This is not necessarily a cheaper solution - the Church Copyright Licence to reproduce song words is currently (2009) £168 per annum for a congregation with an average attendance at its main service of worship of 100 to 249 people. This is not an open licence to print anything but only those songs listed in the agreement. Again, it is worth investigating fully before proceeding – www.ccli.co.uk

Keeping a Check

One of the first things I did when I went to my last parish was to buy a music copy of the hymn book used there at that time - The Church Hymnary Third Edition. Each time we used a hymn from that book I noted the date on the appropriate page. I made a terrible mess of the book, but over the years it became extremely useful in letting me see which hymns we were using regularly, which ones we were doing to death, and which ones we never attempted. Without some such mechanism, which can now be done on your computer, the risk is that we simply keep repeating our own particular favourites and do not make full use of the breadth of choice that is on offer.

Chapter 4

Crafting Worship – Praying

Speaking to God in prayer is such a personal and an emotional thing that it is difficult to think of it in crafting terms. It smacks somehow of manipulation and even deception when what we want above all is honesty and simplicity. But what those of us who dare to lead worship are doing is in fact far from simple - we are endeavouring not just to share our own thoughts and concerns with our God, we are trying to speak on behalf of all those who are present and to represent their interests as well as our own - or perhaps it should be to the exclusion of our own. In a way it is an impossible task because each person at worship has different feelings, different attitudes, and different concerns which they may want to share with God. But that is precisely why I am convinced that praying as part of public worship requires a great deal of crafting. If we are following the practice of the Church of Scotland where the prayers are newly created for each service rather than being taken from an established liturgy, then their preparation requires hours of work rather than minutes. I often found myself taking up to four hours to prepare the two main prayers for Sunday morning worship - Adoration and Confession, Thanksgiving and Intercession. Many worship leaders do not prepare their prayers in advance, believing that the Holy Spirit will inspire their impromptu prayers every bit as much as if they are prepared in advance, and who am I to argue with that position, except to say that it is not for me personally, and that too often I have found that it leads to repetition, lack of structure and disjointed presentation.

So what are the main aspects of crafting prayer for worship?

Simplicity

As I mentioned in chapter 1 language is crucial in worship, but particularly in prayer. If we want to take people with us as we speak to God, then simple thoughts, simply and naturally expressed are always best. If we are trying to impress God with our profundity of thought or breadth of vocabulary there is something wrong with our theology, and if we are trying to impress the congregation in the same ways there is something wrong with us.

Emotion

Simple thoughts, simply expressed does not mean lacking in emotion. One of the challenges and opportunities we all face in leading worship in Scotland is to bring feeling and emotion back into what has too often become a fairly cerebral exercise, and what can be more emotional than the whole idea of coming into the presence of God to offer our worship to him. Over the years I have noticed that while most people can easily produce lists of concerns for the prayers of intercession, and even muster up a few things to be glad about in the thanksgivings, they find it much more difficult to put into words how they feel about God and to express their own inadequacies before him. That is why I particularly like the thought a close friend once shared with me that writing a prayer of adoration should be just "like writing a love letter to God." Our feelings and emotions need to be included in our crafting of prayers.

Structure

As we recognise that people are coming to worship in all sorts of different moods and emotions, we realise that if our prayers are to begin to be meaningful to them, they need to capture and express at least something of that breadth of feeling. The best way I know of doing that is to follow a structure in our prayers, and most denominations produce guidelines to help us do just that in the form of Prayer Books or Books of Common Order. A quick look at the Book of Common Order of the Church of Scotland published in 1994, suggests the well tested formula of two principal prayers within the order for morning worship - Adoration Confession and Supplication early in the service, and Thanksgiving and Intercession towards the end. The hope is that by covering all these moods in our prayers, those who are present will find something to which they can relate however they are feeling and whatever their concerns are. If you are a new Granny delighted at the birth of your grandson, you will surely be in Thanksgiving mode. If you are feeling guilty and regretful about something you have said or done during the last week, the prayers of Confession will help you say sorry to God. If you are worried about the state of our world and the need for peace, the Intercessions will provide a focus for your concerns.

Help!

Crafting prayers for worship week after week, month after month and year after year is a demanding task, and I speak from personal experience when I say that there are two particular problems. One is that awful feeling when we seem to be completely devoid of ideas and cannot get started, especially with the Prayers of Adoration. The other is the equally awful feeling that what we have written is very familiar and probably a close repeat of what we wrote two or three weeks ago. When we hit either of these obstacles, it is time to reach out beyond ourselves and our own limited resources to the great

wealth of material that is available both from the world church today
and from the church through the ages. I have referred in chapter 1 to
a number of resources that are available for worship in general, but
in fact these and many others are probably of most help when it
comes to preparing prayers. Reading other people's prayers can be
particularly helpful - anything from New Moon of the Seasons:
Prayers from the Highlands and Islands collected and translated by
Alexander Carmichael to Gitanjali (Song Offerings) by Rabindranath
Tagore. At the risk of repeating myself let me stress that this is not
so much a matter of importing vast chunks of other people's prayers
into our own as finding a new spark or thought that sends us off
happily in a new direction in our own words.

Chapter 5

Crafting Worship – Preaching

What a nerve! To think that in one chapter I can possibly say anything useful on the huge subject of preaching! But for better or worse here goes - and because it is such a huge subject, I want to come at it simply by giving some hints which have been useful to me and I hope may be helpful to you.

Hint 1 - Be Yourself!

Preaching is a personal thing. Each one of us brings to it everything that makes us who we are and what we are. That is what makes preaching exciting - no two preachers are the same and so no two sermons are the same. So do not be afraid to let yourself show - just as you are, with all your strengths and all your weaknesses. Congregations will appreciate and warm to that far more than either a pretence that you are someone different (pulpit voice!) or a pretence that you are really nobody (I am nothing but a channel for God's word to be heard!) When I hear ministers saying that an argument for wearing robes to lead worship is that it makes the preacher anonymous I wonder what kind of preaching they are thinking about, for to me the essence of preaching lies in you or me helping in our own unique way to bring real people closer to our real

God and there is no way you can do that if you are not being a real person yourself.

Hint 2 - Give God a Break!

I really worry sometimes about what kind of press we are giving God! Is he really so difficult to understand that it takes twenty five or thirty minutes to explain him? Is he really so dull that he can put us to sleep? Is she really so complex that only words like trinitarian and omnipresent can describe her to ordinary people in the pew? Is he really so good that we are left cringing at our own inadequacies? Is she really so powerful that we feel what we do is hardly worth doing? Or is it that we preachers are giving God a bad press? Maybe each one of us who preaches or is preparing to preach needs to ask ourselves what kind of impression we want to convey about the God we serve and the Jesus we follow. Of course it is all Paul's fault because he started the trend to complex theological sermons of considerable length and it has been running ever since! So what about all of us deciding that instead of trying to emulate Paul we should emulate Jesus. And what did Jesus do? Kept it short and kept it simple! Well, he did a few other things as well which helped to heighten his impact, but as far as preaching was concerned he was a master at saying what he wanted to say with the fewest words possible and the simplest words possible.

Hint 3 - Show your Shape!

A sermon needs a shape or a structure. There is nothing wrong with the -

Introduction - Three Main Points - Ending

sort of shape, though there are all sorts of other possibilities and all of us have our own particular favourite. But what we tend to forget is that the main reason for having a structure is not to make it easier for us to write the sermon, but to make it easier for the congregation to listen to it. So why keep it a secret? Tell the congregation what you are doing! Keep them in the picture at each stage in the structure. If there are three things you want to say, people will be focused in their listening if you begin by saying - "There are three things I want to say..." And by ticking them off one by one. If you don't like that kind of shape, but prefer to move forward in a development of your ideas like a straight line, then say so. "This leads me to suggest....." And if your sermon is a circle, there is nothing more helpful than if you openly identify that. "Which brings us back to where we began with the words of Jesus......"

What is much more difficult for the person in the pew to follow is when there appears to be no structure to the sermon that can be easily identified, and one feels like a steel sphere in a pin ball machine, sparking off objects and darting off in a new direction without any apparent reason.

Hint 4 - Start from where people are!

Most sermons succeed or fail in the first thirty seconds. No matter how good your development of your theme is in the main body of the sermon, if you have already lost your listeners it makes no difference. So try to capture their attention at the start! Go to any lengths to do that - tell a joke, produce something ridiculous in the pulpit, refer to Scotland's defeat on the rugby field the previous day (or Rangers or Celtic), do anything that will get the people with you. It is only if you do that first, that you have any chance of introducing them to the astonishing excitements of Habbakuk or Nahum! And when you think about it, that is what good preaching is, not just giving a lecture on some aspect of the Bible, but helping people to discover God in Jesus right where they are in the middle of their daily lives. It is when we do that, and only when we do that, that people will say - "That sermon spoke to me today."

Hint 5 - Get Real!

"It's all very well for you to stand up there, but we've got to get on with living down here." There is a serious risk of a major gulf developing between the world and the lives of people in the world as preachers seem to see it, and the reality of what life in our world today is really like. People who come to Church are already doing something pretty huge in terms of faith and commitment - for all sorts of reasons it is tough to be there, and it is incredibly easy to avoid it. And yet when we do get these faithful folk into the pews, we seem to spend a lot of the time battering them about the head for their failings rather than encouraging them for their witness. Of course we all need to have more faith, to live better lives, to take our discipleship more seriously, to give more money, to spend more time reading our Bibles and saying our prayers. But the reality for us as preachers today is that alongside all of that we have to set the awesome fact that there are still actually people who have come to hear what we have to say. They are living in a world that is complex and difficult to understand and interpret, a world with AIDS and Global Warming and International Terrorism and Third World Poverty and Gun Culture and Financial Meltdown. They need to hear from the pulpit that we recognise the reality of that world, and the enormous difficulties that there are in trying to follow Jesus in that world.

Hint 6 - Lighten Up!

That sounds like a contradiction after Hint 5, but there is no doubt that some of the best sermons I have heard have had a good smattering of humour in them, as well as some appropriate quotes and illustrations. We are asking a lot of people when we expect them to sit and listen to us for fifteen or twenty minutes and one way of sugaring the pill and at the same time reinforcing the message is to tell a story or give a quotation. This is another area where the resources of the Internet, as well as a constantly widening variety of available books, make it much easier to find what we are looking for. Naturally nothing beats an illustration from our own experience, but failing that there is no reason why we cannot use outside resources and personalise them for our particular needs.

I found on the internet this illustration from the American writer Robert Fulghum.

> 'Now let me tell you about Larry Walters, my hero. Walters is a truck driver, thirty three years old. He is sitting in his lawn chair in his backyard, wishing he could fly. For as long as he could remember, he wanted to go *up*. To be able to just rise right up in the air and see for a long way. The time, money, education, and opportunity to be a pilot were not his. Hang gliding was too dangerous, and any good place for gliding was too far away. So he spent a lot of summer afternoons sitting in his backyard in his ordinary old aluminium lawn chair – the kind with the webbing and rivets. Just like the one you've got in your backyard.
>
> The next chapter in this story is carried by the newspapers and television. There's old Larry Walters up in the air over Los Angeles. Flying at last. Really getting UP there. Still sitting in his aluminium lawn chair, but it's hooked on to forty-five helium-filled surplus weather ballons. Larry has a parachute on, a CB radio, a six-pack of beer, some peanut butter and jelly sandwiches, and a BB gun to pop some of the balloons to come down. And instead of being just a couple of hundred feet over his neighbourhood, he shot up eleven thousand feet, right through the approach corridor to the Los Angeles International Airport.
>
> Walters is a taciturn man. When asked by the press why he did it, he said:

"You can't just sit there!" When asked if he was scared, he answered: "Wonderfully so." When asked if he would do it again, he said: "Nope." And asked if he was glad that he did it, he grinned from ear to ear and said: "Oh, yes."

I could not resist using it as the opening of a sermon and the theme is pretty obvious – "You can't just sit there!"

As far as I am concerned there is nothing pleases me more than to have someone say to me, "I really enjoyed the service on Sunday - we had a good laugh." One commentator on Psalm 19 has observed how often the words of the last verse - "Let the words of my mouth and the meditation of my heart be acceptable in thy sight" - have preceded a lengthy, boring and laborious exposition of a biblical passage, yet this particular verse properly understood refers to a song ('the words of my mouth') and the accompanying music ('the reverberation of my heart'). Maybe we need to think a bit more of our sermons as 'songs accompanied by music' and that will help us to "lighten up!"

Hint 7 - The Ideas Box!

One of the most difficult things for a preacher, is to keep coming up with new ideas for sermons. To some extent that problem is solved for those of us who are in the habit of making use of the Lectionary, but that opens us to the risk of turning the sermon into a bible study. If preaching really is about bringing the real God into the real world, then there has to be a spark of inspiration that jumps the gap between and that is where the challenge really lies. The Sermon Ideas Box is one way of trying to face up to that challenge. For many years I have used a brown plastic file box which takes 6 x 4 lined filing cards with a label stuck on the outside which says - "Sermon Ideas". Whenever something crops up which I think might have the potential to be worked up into a sermon, I jot down on a blank card as many details as I can and file it away in the box. As I mentioned previously this happens more often than not when I am doing my daily bible study, but as all of us know ideas can come from all sorts of sources - a programme on TV, a news item in the newspaper, an article in a magazine, a passage in a book, a conversation with a neighbour - the list is endless. If like me, you do some of your best thinking in the middle of the night, keep a supply of cards and a pen in your bedside drawer and force yourself to jot down something there and then, even if it is just one word that will remind you in the morning of that brilliant idea you had at 4 am. There is nothing more frustrating than to know that you had the perfect ending for Sunday's sermon all worked out in the middle of the night, and now you cannot remember it!

Chapter 6

Crafting Worship – Sharing and Enabling

Like any other organisation or institution fashions come and go in the Church. There is no doubt that one of the current fashions is for the involvement and participation of church members in leading worship, so much so that any Service which does not have members of the congregation taking an active part is doomed in the eyes of many. Of course I am not suggesting that there are not sound theological reasons to support it, but like all fashions there is good and bad in this particular one, and we need to think very carefully before jumping on the bandwagon. Here are some of the issues which I believe we have to take into consideration.

a) One of the purposes of training clergy biblically and theologically is so that they can share what they have learnt with their congregations. If we are to take advantage of this resource there need to be times when we listen to what they have to say.

b) Even the most carefully crafted and imaginative act of worship loses something if it is led entirely by one person.

c) We have to guard against the "participation at any price" ethic. Basic things like audibility really matter and no congregation is comfortable if the person leading worship is in an agony of nerves.

d) Real participation, as distinguished from tokenism (a lay person reading the Old Testament lesson?) is hard work and demands a lot of time and preparation from everybody.

e) Every congregation has someone who is only too eager to volunteer to help lead the worship but we do need to ask ourselves what their motives are and whether these motives are good.

So where does that take us? My own view is that what we should *not* be doing in the name of participation, is simply handing out tasks to members of the congregation - "You read a Lesson *here*, and you say a prayer *here*." Our role as clergy has to be much more than simply being the stage manager in a production. What we should be doing is working with people to enable them to make a genuine and personal contribution to the worship of the congregation. That may mean in some cases rehearsing a bible reading with them in the sanctuary (including familarising them with the sound system) so that they are enabled to take part to the best of their ability, while in others giving help and guidance in the difficult task of writing a prayer.

It may be helpful to recognise two distinct levels of participation both of which have their own validity. The first is where the role of the clergy person is to prepare a script for an act of worship, for example on Christmas Sunday, and then to choose suitable people in the congregation to bring that script to life with all the necessary rehearsal that involves. That is demanding enough but the second level is even more demanding - to gather together a group of people (worship group) and think through with them the theme for a service of worship, then to develop that theme through all the different parts of the service. The role of the clergy person in this context will depend on the gifts and abilities of the people involved. Those who are most confident about their own abilities in writing a prayer for example, may be the ones who need the most help!

There is no doubt that the participation of members of the congregation can add greatly to the effectiveness and value of worship both for those who are taking part and those who form the congregation. There is no doubt also that enabling participation in a genuine way is extremely demanding of the minister - it is never an easy way of getting a Sunday off!

Chapter 7

Crafting Worship – Breaking the Mould

One of the most exciting experiences I have had in crafting worship, has been to abandon all the customary orders of service and liturgies and to start with a completely clean sheet of paper, or rather a completely blank hour. Of course it is not possible nor would it be desirable to do that every Sunday, but I am sure that there are times when a particular topic or theme lends itself to that kind of radical approach. In other words what I am suggesting is that sometimes the theme should determine the form and order of the service, rather than being pushed into a predetermined structure which is what we would normally do. My own experience is that for some reason this works particularly well on special festivals and occasions when a fresh approach may be particularly welcome. I have always felt for example that worship on Good Friday which is made up of the usual "sandwich" of praise, prayers, readings and sermon, fails to capture the unique nature and message of this special day in the church's life. One very simple way is to put together a service made up of readings which tell the story and meaning of Good Friday, interspersed with suitable items of praise, rather along the lines of the traditional Service of Nine Lessons and Carols at Christmas. But that is still a fairly traditional structure which hardly makes Good Friday impinge on our lives. One approach I have taken is to structure a service around the simple objects involved in the crucifixion itself with suitable voices, readings and music - the wine, the hammer and nails, the crown of thorns, and the spear. You will find an outline of this service in Appendix B. Another approach is to use the familiar words of Psalm 121 - "I to the hills will lift mine eyes" and of the Hymn "There is a green hill far away" to create a Service which develops the significance of hills in the life of Jesus. The first hill is Golgotha representing Sacrifice; the second is the hill on which Mark records that Jesus chose his twelve disciples representing Challenge; the third hill is the one on which Jesus preached the Sermon on the Mount representing Devotion; the fourth hill is the one in Galilee where Jesus issued his great commission - "Go then to all peoples everywhere and make them my disciples..." representing Mission; and the worship ends by focusing again on the hill of Good Friday. In this way the events of Good Friday help us to reflect on the meaning of the whole life of Jesus and its impact on us. You will find an outline of this service in Appendix C. A third and even more radical approach which some might find even offensive takes the theme of "Laughing at God" to explore the different and sometimes cruel ways in which we laugh at each other and the different and sometimes cruel ways in which people laughed at Jesus, climaxing in the laughter of the soldiers at the foot of the cross and the laughter of the passers-by as they hurled abuse. "He saved others, but he cannot save himself. Let the Messiah, the king of Israel, come down from the cross." The Service ends with these words:

"There is a choice. There is the possibility of laughing with God rather than laughing at God, of laughing with sheer amazement at all He has done for us on this day, which after all we call GOOD Friday; of laughing with the relief of knowing that we have been saved from ourselves; of laughing with delight at the knowledge that this is not the end but the beginning."

You will find an outline of this service in Appendix D.

Good Friday is just one opportunity to take a more creative approach by "breaking the mould." Another is that instead of moaning about how early the celebration of Christmas begins every year and how commercialised it has become, to seize the opportunity which the Christian Year gives us as Christians to properly recognise Advent as our lead up to Christmas in worship. The planning and presentation of an Advent Theme which takes place as part of the Service (perhaps replacing the normal children's slot) on the four Sundays of Advent, gives the people of the Church a real feeling of anticipation about the coming of Christmas and the birth of Jesus. The possibilites are limited only by your imagination! A Christmas pudding with four slices, four enormous gold bells hung from the roof of the church, a giant Advent candle, an Advent calendar with opening doors and windows to reveal appropriate gifts, and a full-size nativity scene which is occupied over the four Sundays by the participants in the nativity story, are just some of the ideas which can be developed, and can create opportunities for genuine participation both in the Advent theme itself by adults and children, and in the preparation and making of the necessary props. You will find outlines for some Advent Themes in Appendix E.

Of course there is no reason why we should not try "breaking the mould" on ordinary Sundays as well as high days and holy days! But Advent and Christmas, Holy Week and Easter, Pentecost and Harvest Thanksgiving do seem to provide special opportunities. We do have to bear in mind however that this kind of Service is not everyone's cup of tea and be prepared that while some will find a new and creative experience of worship on Good Friday inspiring and moving, others will protest that "there was no sermon"! That is why it is particularly important that when we are "breaking the mould" we keep those who are worshipping fully informed of what we are doing. A worship leaflet with a detailed order of service is essential, and this can be enhanced by words of explanation at the beginning of the service and at each stage in its development. If people understand the *letter* of what is happening they are much more likely to join in the *spirit*!

It is possible to break the mould using materials produced by others rather than writing a full script ourselves, though there is inevitably a loss of immediacy. Once again there is a great deal of material available. One of the most moving worship experiences of recent years for me has been to use "The *ALTER*nativity Advent Meal" (published by *ALTER*nativity & Wild Goose Resource Group) including all the details down to the mince and tatties and glass of wine. It really is "a different Christmas celebration."

It is almost inevitable that for example a Healing Service produced for use in Iona Abbey will not necessarily work so well in the local church setting. In practice I have found that using a combination of my own material and material "borrowed" from others works very well, though we have to pay attention to the question of copyright. But I would also encourage every worship leader, at least once in their ministry, to throw away the order of service, start with a blank hour and take the risk of "breaking the mould." You may be surprised at the response you get as well as the sense of satisfaction you experience!

Chapter 8

Crafting Worship – Children versus Adults

There is a familiar saying - "If it's not broken, don't fix it." I wonder sometimes if we are in danger of trying to do just that in relation to the difficult question of involving both children and adults in worship. There has been a tradition which probably goes back to Victorian times of having a bit at the beginning of the service for children who then leave for Sunday School while the worship continues at a more adult level. If you want to be "politically correct" today you will reject this approach in favour of a more "inclusive" approach which includes everyone from babes in arms to geriatrics. The Family Service and All Age Worship are laudable attempts to do just that and along with everyone else I have done my best to make the vision a reality. The trouble is that in my experience it is an extremely difficult thing to do and what so often happens is that we finish up with a service which is really for children and has little in it that appeals to adults beyond smiling at the antics of the wee ones. Making it possible for children to worship rather than getting them to put on an entertainment is such a difficult thing to achieve on its own without combining it with trying to cater for adults as well. So I am left wondering if maybe our predecessors had it right - a slot for the children at the beginning and then continue for the adults?

The jury is still very much out on that one, but it is interesting that some churches who have introduced all-age worship on particular Sundays have found that the attendance has dropped on these occasions, and that very few congregations have entirely abandoned the "old fashioned" slot for the children at the start. But if we are going to continue with that approach we do need to look very carefully at what we do in that slot to ensure that it offers a genuine worship experience for our kids. All too often the so-called Children's Address is anything but that. Sometimes it is used simply to break the ice with the adults, sometimes it offers a trailer for the sermon, and sometimes it is an opportunity for fun and games. There is nothing wrong with any of these, but they are not quite hitting the target of a short act of worship for children - a suitable song; a prayer in language that children understand and ideas that children relate to; a talk, address, message or activity which is bible related and expresses some aspect of the Christian faith; and a second suitable song. Of course it is true that this divides the service into two parts - the first for children and the second for adults - but I am not convinced there is anything wrong with that if it is done carefully. I am sure that there are few adults who will find fault with having to sit through the bit for the children and experience shows that they usually enjoy it for what it is.

"Any ideas for a Children's Address?" Anyone who leads worship regularly is all too familiar with the question and one of the more interesting sociological phenomena of the modern world is how quickly a good idea for a Children's Address can sweep across the country from coast to coast usually immediately after a group of ministers have been attending a conference at Crieff Hydro! This is where it helps to have a theme for the whole Service whether you are following the Lectionary or not, because the Children's Address can be an integral part of the worship rather than a totally isolated event. Once again there are lots of resources for those weeks when you are stuck for an idea. I have found old favourites like "Something To

Say to the Children" by John Gray and "Talks for Children" by Beatrice Surtees and Ian MacLeod helpful at such times, as well as esermons.com but there are many others.

I am not sure if any research has been done on how successful the health warnings are on cigarette packets but I would like to put a health warning on Children's Addresses - not so much for the "consumer" as for the "presenter." It would read something like this - "Danger - Risk of Moralising and Finger Wagging". We want to share with our children the incredible graciousness of our God as we meet him in Jesus but for some reason when we talk to them we very often seem to get side-tracked into giving them a lecture about "being good." I am sure that kids need to be told not to tell lies, not to cheat at exams, not to bash their classmates around the head, not to throw stones at old folks' windows and so on, but there is surely a higher priority for those few precious minutes on a Sunday morning.

Chapter 9

Crafting Worship – Celebrating

One of the things my wife feels very strongly about is that birthdays, anniversaries, and other special occasions should not be glossed over or forgotten but celebrated appropriately! As you can imagine that means we have had some great parties over the years, the best of all being an evening cruise on Loch Lomond with family and friends to mark our joint retirements. The Church is in a unique position because we do not have to look for excuses to celebrate - Christmas and Easter belong to us, and not just these two but all the other great festivals of the Christian Year. On top of that there are special occasions occurring all through the year which are good reason for celebration. We even use the words "There will be a *celebration* of Holy Communion.........." and "The Sacrament of Baptism will be *celebrated*....." when we announce them in advance.

The trouble is that when it comes to the day itself we seem to have some serious hang-ups about making worship celebration. It probably stems from the false idea that being Presbyterian and Reformed means ignoring the great High Days and Holy Days of the Church and still survives for example in the reaction we sometimes get to having candles lit for worship. So although we use the word "celebrate" it does not always feel like a celebration, and all of us at one time or another have attended a Communion Service which felt more like a funeral than a party! I am not suggesting that we should turn Communion into a 'happy clappy' dancing-in-the-aisles occasion but surely it is possible to 'loosen up' just a little.

How to begin? That is easy - simply recognise that there are special days and special occasions as part of the church's life. I am surprised at how few churches give any recognition to Advent as a way of preparing for Christmas, and likewise how few churches fully recognise the opportunity which Holy Week offers us to follow in the foosteps of Jesus in these final days of his life on earth. Of course we cannot expect to move immediately from no services in Holy Week to full churches every evening. Changes like these take time and patience. But we need to begin somewhere, by acknowledging these days for celebration. And what about Pentecost? Surely the forgotten festival of the reformed churches but what an opportunity, excuse even, to do something different. After all it is not every day that we can justify total chaos in the church – complete with tongues of fire and rushing wind!

How to continue? That is easy too. Just ask yourself what was good about your last birthday and most people would answer that it was different from all the other days. It was special! That is what we need to aim at in the Church - making worship on these particular days different and special. There are lots of ways of doing that - an orchestra or band to lead the praise, a special preacher to give the sermon, a group from the congregation to dramatise the action, or simply decorating the church in such a way that it is clear something special is happening. The possibilities are endless, once we begin to celebrate!

Chapter 10

Pastoral Care –
What's It All About?

If worship is the French polishing of ministrycraft then pastoral care is the cabinet making! Because of the links between my former congregation in Bridge of Allan and Charles Rennie Mackintosh I have had a number of opportunities over the years to work with skilled craftsmen on the restoration and development of different aspects of the Mackintosh furniture in that building. What impressed me most was the time, patience and attention to detail that was involved as well as the skill, to ensure that the end result was right. Pastoral care is like that. It makes huge demands in time, it requires endless patience, there are no short cuts, it needs the best of our skills and abilities both natural and learnt, and the end result may often reveal little of the attention to detail that has gone into it.

Pastoral Care - Why Do We Do It?

So why do we do it? Is it just because there is an expectation which has to be fulfilled? Is it because as ministers we want to avoid the kind of criticism that can arise in congregations that "the minister never visits!"? There must be a better reason than just to keep our noses clean but before we explore that, it is important to identify exactly what we are talking about when we speak of "pastoral care." What we are *not* talking about, is blanket visiting of the congregation or the parish by either the minister or members of the congregation.

That may be good public relations especially in a new ministry, it may be one way of tackling mission outreach, but it is not pastoral care. Pastoral care is more than getting to know people, it is different from inviting people to come to church. As its name implies it is one person caring and looking after another, just as the shepherd cares for and looks after his sheep. That image helps to answer the question "Why do we do it?" because it brings to mind one of the most familiar and striking images of Jesus in the Gospels encapsulated in his words - "I am the good shepherd." (John 10 : 11) Not to put too fine a point on it, pastoral care is something we do as Christians because Jesus did it. His whole ministry was filled with concern for others and much of what he did was in response to situations where people were suffering in one way or another. He made real the love of God for them. It is my belief that if we are seeking to follow Jesus and to be his disciples, a large part of that means we seek to follow his example of love and concern. We are called by Jesus to try to make real the love of God to those around us, and that call is encapsulated for us in these words of Jesus - "My commandment is this: love one another, just as I love you." (John 15: 12)

That means that we are giving a very significant status to pastoral care. If this is such an important part of our discipleship it is not something that we can do if we have the time, or only if there are not other more important things to do. I would say that along with preparation for and participating in worship, it is *the* most important thing we do as ministers of the gospel, and it concerns me that ministry today does not always give full credence to that position. It also means that we are privileged in the Church to do something for people that is quite different from medical care or social work care or any other kind of care. When we visit someone who is ill on behalf of the Church, we are personalising and making real the love of God for them - that is a huge privilege and a tremendous responsibility. There is a sense then in which pastoral care is sacramental - it is a physical expression of the pastoral care of Jesus, and a symbol of the loving care of God.

Pastoral Care - Who Does the Caring?

If as I have suggested this is an important part of our discipleship then it follows that all of us, ministers, elders and church members are called to share in pastoral care. That gives the lie to the impression we often get in the church that pastoral care is the job of the minister, while the congregation's role is to be on the receiving end of his or her ministrations! That is not just bad theology, it is a recipe for disaster, as no minister can possibly give pastoral support in any adequate sense to several hundred people. What instead we have to aim for is a structure of pastoral care in which everyone in the family of the church has a part to play and which recognises the gifts and skills that each one of us has to offer, as well as the particular needs of those whom we seek to care for.

There is no perfect model for pastoral care but it may be helpful to share with you one that experience has shown to work well. The basic premise that lies behind it is that what could be called the ongoing, non-acute pastoral care of those who are elderly and housebound or suffering from long-term illness is undertaken primarily by district elders through their regular visits to all the members in their districts, supplemented when appropriate by more frequent visits by trained church visitors drawn from the membership of the congregation. The primary role of the minister and anyone else involved such as the pastoral assistant or probationer minister in some congregations, is the pastoral care of those in acute and crisis situations - those who are in hospital, are very ill, are approaching death, or are recently bereaved. This is not to suggest that the second group is more important than the first. It is simply a recognition that the more acute needs can usually best be met through a minister or pastoral assistant who is trained and available to respond immediately. Nor is it to suggest that the boundaries are hard and fast - on the contrary, a good district elder or church visitor will want to visit when someone they care for is in hospital as well as the minister. Hopefully also, the freeing up of the minister's pastoral time which should occur if such a set-up is working well, will enable him or her to take the opportunity perhaps once or twice a year, to visit those who fall into the ongoing, non - acute group.

Pastoral Care - How Is It Organised?

There are a number of computerised systems for organising pastoral care using software which has been specially designed for the purpose. I have to confess that I have not used any of these, mainly because I consider one of the key elements in any good system of pastoral care has to be that you can take the person's details with you, and doing a round of visits clutching a batch of A4 computer print-out seemed inappropriate to say the least! The advent of notebooks and pocket PCs has changed all that and made it possible to carry pastoral information with you which you can access at any time. I have used 5" x 3" index cards which are big enough to hold quite a lot of information but small enough to be discreet and slip into a pocket or handbag. The card contains a note of the person's name, address and phone number at the top and thereafter is simply a record of the visits made. This can have three elements - the date of the visit, the name or initials or code of the person visiting, and a few words of detail about the circumstances and possibly the visit. So a pastoral card might look something like this:

Brown, Mrs Isa		Tel 01234 567890
27 Hill Street		
Anytown		
10 Aug 08	Visited in ERI – Ward 16	JCN
	Hernia op tomorrow – cheery	
17 Aug 08	Home – doing well	MKS
31 Aug 08	Getting out – concern about	JCN
	daughter's marriage	

There are a number of advantages to a card system like this. The most obvious is that we are not relying on our memories to retain a lot of information about a lot of people, with the risk that someone gets forgotten. The second is that if we are working in a "team" situation information can be easily shared. Either the card can be passed to another member of the team or preferably he or she can make out a card too so that each person involved in the care has a complete picture of the pastoral needs of the congregation. This is specially useful in an emergency, or if one member of the team is not available because of holidays or illness.

The obvious disadvantage, and one that has to be taken very seriously, is that as soon as we write down personal details about people, we have to be extremely careful to maintain confidentiality. It has been my practice to use a small file box of "active" cards with separation index cards which identify for example those who are in one particular hospital or care home. That box has to be constantly in my possession, and never left lying around either in the church office or hall, or at home. In the same way, "inactive" cards which will build up over the years to a very substantial quantity, need to be carefully stored in a lockable card index box, preferably metal, which is kept in the church office or the minister's study. Arising from that, a further advantage of the card system becomes clear - that when someone requires pastoral care who has been ill previously perhaps several years ago, the carer can be reminded immediately of the details of that previous illness by extracting the individual's card from the locked "inactive" storage box.

The other very considerable advantage of a card system is that it is relatively quick and easy to identify how long it is since a person has been visited, and to make use of that information in deciding priorities. A development of that in relation to the ongoing visiting of elderly, housebound and people with long-term illness, is to use divider cards in your pastoral box for each month of the year and to distribute the cards for these individuals over the year. The idea then is that during the month of January the carer will visit the people whose cards are in the January section, and so on throughout the calendar year. Once a person has been visited, you can decide how soon you feel a further visit should be made and slot them into the system accordingly. For example when you visit an elderly person in April, you may discover that she is less well than when last visited, and feel that it would be good to visit her again in two months rather than four months as previously, so following the visit you would slot her card into the section for June.

If more than one person is involved in the acute pastoral care within a congregation, it is essential that the team meets regularly, preferably weekly. This weekly meeting provides an opportunity to report on those who have been visited during the previous week (enabling pastoral cards to be updated) and to decide who will be visited during the coming week and by whom. This will depend very much on local circumstances and the members of the team. In my last charge I was fortunate to work in close liaison with the church's pastoral assistant who was fully trained. As a result we were able to share equally in the pastoral work and decide at the weekly meeting which of us would visit members in hospital that week, while the other would perhaps focus on other situations in the home, such as follow-up visits to a bereavement and funeral service. Sharing the load in this way meant that minister and pastoral assistant could share concerns in confidence at the weekly meeting, and that those being cared for were used to and comfortable with a visit from either minister or pastoral assistant, so that if there was a sudden change either could respond immediately and effectively. It also meant that the distinctive pastoral gifts of each member of the team could be used in the most appropriate way. This might mean that minister and pastoral assistant might alternate weekly in one situation, while ongoing visiting by the pastoral assistant alone or the minister alone might be best in another situation.

If all of this sounds like a lot of work, then it is! How much work we put into not just our pastoral care but the effective organisation of our pastoral care is an indication of how seriously we take it. A minister who states openly that he or she visits pastorally if he or she has time, is sending a very strong message to the people in the church not just about his or her level of concern for them, but about how much (or how little!) the church cares about them.

Pastoral Care - What is a Church Visitor?

As ministers we are constantly emphasising to our people how important it is that their Christian faith finds expression in action, and particularly in showing love and concern for those who are in need in one way or another. The Parable of the Good Samaritan which begins with the question - "Who is my neighbour?" and ends with Jesus saying to every one of us, "You go, then, and do the same" is an opportunity that we preachers welcome to press home the importance of showing love as an integral part of our discipleship. Usually the sermon stops just when it is beginning to get interesting - at the point where the preacher needs to explain in practical terms how that kind of love and care can be put to work in the church today. Inviting members to serve as Church Visitors within a congregation takes Christian love and care into a reality where it can actually stop being a nice but vague feeling of concern, and start being positive action.

Once again there are a number of different models of Church Visitor Scheme but whatever way it is organised it will function best if two key elements are fulfilled. The first is that it should be on a one-to-one basis. In other words, one visitor to one member. This is important because it sets a realistic expectation of time and commitment for those who are undertaking this service, and because it makes it possible to set a level of contact which is going to be beneficial and not just tokenism. We would all agree that for a Church Visitor to call on an elderly, housebound person only once or twice a year probably does more harm than good. If we are serious about this, then it is not unreasonable to suggest to Church Visitors that at least once a month, and preferably once a fortnight is an appropriate level of visiting to begin to meet the needs of those who are being ministered to. We can ask for and accept that level of commitment when the Church Visitor has one person to visit. If we start to load them down with a whole list of people, then the commitment becomes too great, the people being visited feel neglected, the Church Visitor feels guilty at not fulfiling his or her role, and the system founders with hurt on all sides. It also in most congregations of even moderate size indicates the scale of the need that exists - you may be surprised and the congregation may be surprised to discover that the appeal for Church Visitors is looking for thirty or even fifty volunteers rather than eight or twelve.

The second key element in a good Church Visitor Scheme is training. If we are asking people to undertake this new and challenging role, then we need to give them the tools for the job. An initial training session before Church Visitors begin work is essential to address issues like "What to say on your first visit" and "How to get past discussing the weather." It also needs to deal with important practical issues like Identification Cards or Badges and arrangements for feed-back of information. But training should not just be a one-off exercise at the beginning. It should be ongoing, perhaps once a year or every other year, so that Church Visitors can be refreshed in their task and reminded of its importance. It is not difficult to find suitable topics for training sessions on an ongoing basis. A health visitor from the local Health Centre might give a talk on hypothermia. Information on DSS Benefits could be the focus at another. Since many of those being visited will inevitably be elderly, Church Visitors will require support in dealing with bereavement. One topic which requires to be mentioned at every training session is the crucial one of confidentiality and we shall look at this topic in more detail in the last section of this chapter.

The best way of setting up and running a Church Visitor Scheme is to find someone with good administrative skills and pastoral sensitivity to act as Coordinator. It is the Coordinator's job to maintain an accurate and up-to-date record of the Church Visitors and the people whom they are visiting, and again this is probably best done with a card system. The Church Visitor Coordinator can also be heavily involved in organising training sessions and can provide a first point of contact for Visitors who may be experiencing difficulty or feeling inadequate for the task. However it is important to emphasise that the Coordinator should not be left on his or her own to undertake the two crucial tasks on which the welfare of a Church Visitor Scheme depends - identifying those who will be visited by the Church Visitors, and pairing those to be visited with suitable Visitors. Both of these jobs require full input from the minister and/or pastoral team along with the Coordinator, and once again confidentiality is extremely important. When the Scheme is first being set up both these tasks will take a lot of time and hard work by those involved to make sure that as far as possible the pairings are suitable. For example, you might feel that it is not the right time to ask a person who has just lost their mother to cancer and who has taken the first step out of bereavement by volunteering as a Church Visitor to visit someone who is also suffering from cancer. However it may be that at a later stage this same Church Visitor will be exactly the right person to give support when cancer is diagnosed.

Pastoral Care - Confidentiality

The importance of confidentiality in pastoral care has already been touched on, but requires further consideration. As a society we are becoming more aware that information about people cannot just be handed out in a completely uncontrolled way, and the Church is not exempt from such legal requirements as The Data Protection Act. But what is much more important is that if we are seeking to care for people in the name of Jesus and as an expression of the love of God for them, the last thing we want to do is to upset or hurt them by revealing confidential information about them to other people. This means that at every level of pastoral care - keeping records, arranging visits, and pastoral team meetings - the greatest care needs to be taken to ensure that confidentiality is respected. There are two golden rules in this respect - only pass on the information that is absolutely essential to fulfil the pastoral role; and if in doubt ask the person concerned for permission to pass on their details. If you feel this is being overstated it is worth noting that hospitals will no longer give out the names of patients, far less the nature of their illness. It is not difficult to think of examples where passing on information can be damaging. The minister finds a member in hospital who has a liver problem caused by excessive drinking. The minister then phones the District Elder who immediately visits the member in hospital and talks about the member's illness. The member is embarrassed that the elder knows about his problem, and angry that what was felt to be confidential information has been passed on. When it comes to equally emotive situations such as gynaecological procedures, the diagnosis of cancer, and mental health problems, it becomes clear why confidentiality is so important. It goes without saying that this applies not just to the minister but to pastoral assistants, church visitors and anyone who is involved in pastoral care within the church.

Chapter 11

Pastoral Care – The Next Steps

You might be forgiven for thinking that so far all I have said about pastoral care has been very much inward focused, and that would largely be true. No matter how all-encompassing we would like to be in our care for others, we also have to be practical and recognise that if we are going to minister effectively then there do have to be boundaries. While no minister worthy of the name would ever refuse to offer help when requested by someone outwith the congregation or parish, it is unwise and presumptuous of us to be proactive in promoting ourselves as all singing, all dancing, all problem solving, all times, all situations, and all people Super-Pastors! But that does not mean we can do nothing - just that what we try to do has to be just as well organised and carefully planned as always. All of us in the Church today must be concerned about the human problems men and women and children are facing in their lives, and all of us wonder what we can do about it. Again, I would offer not the final answer by any means but one model that has worked in a small way and might be helpful to others.

Community Visitors

If we have members of the Church who having been suitably trained to visit regularly and offer care to other members of the Church on an ongoing one-to-one basis, can we not extend this idea beyond the confines of the congregation into the community? A Community Visitor Scheme aims to do just that - to offer a Visitor to people in the community who may have no connection with any Church but have a need for such a service. The difficulty is how to identify such people and how to avoid the obvious pitfalls of making them feel they are charitable cases on the one hand or the raw material for religious conversion on the other. In our particular situation the way in which we achieved this was through a good working relationship with our local health care centre. In discussion with GPs, District Nurses and Health Visitors, it became clear that there were people in the community who were in need of something more than the health care services were able to offer. Comments like "She badly needs someone to talk to" and "He never speaks to another man" and the sense of frustration felt by nurses and health visitors that they could not spend more time with certain people, led to the idea that the Church, and in our case several congregations working together, could provide suitably trained Community Visitors who would meet this need for "befriending" on a one-to-one basis. One difficulty which was identified early on, was that while it is relatively easy to visit a church member for the first time simply by identifying yourself as being from "St Andrew's Church", visiting in the community requires a more careful approach and a more concrete form of identification. This was achieved by appointing a Community Visitor Coordinator who liaised with staff in the Health Care Team to pair Community Visitors with potential "customers." Once this had been done and the name of the Visitor was known, the District Nurse or Health Visitor, on their next visit, would discuss with their patient the possibility of them having a regular Community Visitor. If they agreed, they would be given one part of the Community Visitor Scheme Card which would carry the name of their Community Visitor. Having been given the all clear to begin visiting, the Community Visitor, would make his or her first visit, using the other part of the Community Visitor Scheme Card as identification on the door step. This meant that no one was put in the position of receiving a visit "cold" from some anonymous do-gooder from the church, and that no one would be visited unless they had already agreed. In practice the Scheme worked well, though on a relatively small scale. As with Church Visitors two key elements were ongoing training of the Visitors, and regular meetings to review the Scheme. Two things in particular were emphasised to all concerned, that this was a service offered by the Church to the community in the name of Jesus and that there was no question of it being an attempt to fill the pews in the local church; and that Community Visitors were offering friendship and support and were not substituting for the health care professionals. What became clear, even in a relatively affluent community, was the extent of the need for caring of this kind for people of all ages and backgrounds.

The Ministry of Flowers

One of the ways in which the love and concern of the Church can be expressed for someone is through the ministry of flowers. I refer of course to the flowers which in most churches are placed in the sanctuary each Sunday. How that is organised, where the flowers are put in the church, and different ways of meeting the cost are not my chief concern at this point, but what is done with the flowers afterwards can be an important part of our pastoral care. I myself have on a number of occasions been on the receiving end of the flowers from the Church - family bereavement and personal illness - so I can testify at first hand as to just how important this part of our pastoral care can be. It is not the number or value or even the condition of the flowers that matters - It Is the message they convey to the recipient that in this time of crisis or need the Church is concerned for them and caring for them and that means God in Jesus is concerned for them and caring for them. It is such a simple thing to do, but its impact is enormous. What is particularly good about it is that in situations where we all struggle and fail to find the right words, no words are needed here, beyond the simple statement - "These are the church flowers for you." The flowers themselves say all that needs to be said.

Because I am convinced this is more than just a "nice thing to do" and is central to the Church's pastoral care rather than on the periphery, I believe that it does need attention and effort if it is to realise its full potential. First of all it is important that the minister or a member of the pastoral team who is fully conversant with the pastoral situation in the congregation and community should make the important decision about who should receive the flowers each Sunday. This makes it possible to send the flowers in bereavement, illness, or other distressing circumstance which may not be widely known. Second, we need to encourage those who deliver the flowers to recognise the significance of what they are doing, for in that moment on the doorstep they represent and personify the Church. As they hand over that bunch of flowers, they are in a real sense offering nothing less than the love of Jesus when it is needed most. Third, from a practical point of view it is helpful for everyone involved to have a simple card with a suitable message, on the reverse of which the name and address of the recipient of the flowers can be written. Finally, experience has shown that it is very useful to keep a "Flower Book" which records the recipients of the flowers each Sunday. Otherwise we can very easily find ourselves asking - "Did we send the flowers two weeks ago to Mr Brown in the hospital?" This is particularly important when we want to send the flowers to members of the congregation who are housebound or suffering from long-term illness - the "Flower Book" enables us to check on when they were last recipients and whether there might be someone else who could be regarded as a priority. Of course the "Flower Book" could be kept in the form of file cards and if the "Who Got the Flowers When" information is cross-referenced onto the pastoral cards as already described in chapter 10, this can be extremely helpful when assessing priority at the weekly pastoral meeting.

Harvest, Christmas and Easter

Most churches have long since discontinued the practice of sending harvest gifts to members of the congregation on the grounds that no one today in our country is really in need. Instead they have substituted a variety of ways of giving where there is genuine need either in our own country or the third world. But while it is true that the material need has gone, other needs are probably greater than ever. Even in relatively well-off communities where our churches are strongest, elderly people live alone and can be very lonely, and young couples can feel isolated and without roots. Each one of us can be caught up in illness, unemployment, the breakdown of marriage or relationships, problems with children, or bereavement.

The good thing about getting a Harvest Gift from the Church was that even if you did not need it you knew that someone somewhere knew you and cared about you enough to send you half a dozen eggs, a turnip and two carrots! There is no reason why we cannot continue that positive aspect of Harvest Festival by delivering a small bunch of flowers or even better a potted plant, to those whom the Pastoral Team identifies as appropriate recipients. Naturally this involves the cost of purchasing the flowers or plants, but this can easily be met by making it part of the Harvest Appeal. Once again a simple message on a card will enhance the meaning of the gift. A potted plant has the advantage that it will last more than a week or so. "That's my plant from the Church! It's six months since I got it and look at it!" And once again members of the congregation are invited to be part of the church's pastoral ministry by delivering the plants. What about suggesting to the congregation as I did, that the gifts be delivered on a one-to-one basis - which meant we needed around a hundred volunteers? There was no doubt of the "feel good" factor for everyone involved when it worked!

There is good reason to consider applying the same kind of approach both at Christmas and Easter. Even those who are not regular attenders at worship seem to get something out of coming to church at Christmas and Easter, so it is not difficult to imagine how difficult it is if you have been a regular attender and are no longer able to be present. Many congregations have acknowledged this need by introducing schemes whereby audio or even video recordings of church services are circulated to those who are housebound. But it is worth considering whether those who are on the pastoral list might receive a poinsettia at Christmas or a small bunch of daffodils at Easter, along with an appropiate card and greeting. There is no way of measuring the value such a relatively inexpensive gift might have in a particular situation. In addition there is a valuable "learning curve" for all those involved in preparing, organising and delivering the gifts, and many opportunities for the involvement of all age groups. Just as one example, children could participate by designing a suitable card to be delivered with the gifts.

One final point in relation to the ministry of flowers is that much of the tedious and time - consuming task of writing names and addresses on cards can be overcome by the use of printed computer labels and the computerised congregational data base. A suitable label can be devised which has for example a Christmas logo and message as well as the name and address of the recipient.

Chapter 12

Worship and Pastoral Care – The Link

This book so far has had two very definite and apparently distinct themes - Worship and Pastoral Care. Most of the time we see these as two very different functions of ministry. The purpose of this chapter is to explore ways in which a developing ministry of pastoral care leads into worship, so that the two are linked together in a relationship that is inter-dependent.

A period of Study Leave in late 1998 gave me the opportunity to stop and think about the way in which our pastoral ministry was developing and where it might be leading us. The structure which was in place at that time involved a weekly pastoral meeting between the minister, pastoral assistant and probationer minister to report on the previous week's pastoral work and to plan for the coming week: a team of twenty five church visitors keeping in touch with members of the congregation on a one-to-one basis; a second team of twelve community visitors working in a similar way in the community in cooperation with other local churches and the health care team; and over forty district elders maintaining contact with all members of the congregation four times a year. The minister and Pastoral Assistant focused on "crisis" visiting in hospital, at home and in the context of bereavement, and following up on situations of concern passed on by church and community visitors and district elders, though also maintaining an ongoing programme of visits to the longer term elderly or ill in residential establishments, sheltered housing, and at home. Following discussion at Kirk Session it was agreed that when the Pastoral Team became aware of a member in hospital, they would pass that information as soon as possible to the District Elder if they did not already know. In this way District Elders who wished to do so were able to play a fuller role in the pastoral care of their people.

While it might be thought that with such a structure in place, and assuming it worked well, our pastoral care programme was satisfactory, a number of factors seemed to suggest otherwise. These were first a tendency which developed without any conscious decision on our part for both the minister and pastoral assistant to be increasingly involved in situations where someone was very ill and/or someone was dying. Perhaps this is best explained by giving an example.

A lady in middle age suffering from an unusual genetic disorder whom we had visited regularly for years, deteriorated gradually, was admitted to the local general hospital, and subsequently transferred to a city hospital. Her condition worsened and the decision was eventually taken to switch off her life-support systems. The pastoral assistant and I visited this lady almost every day for a period of five weeks and I was present with her husband when she died.

Out of this situation and a number of similar ones a strong feeling developed on our part that we would like to do more than be there with people and/or pray with them and for them, but that some more distinctive ministry was required both for the person concerned and for his/her immediate family, both at the time of death and at a later stage once the formalities including the funeral had been completed.

The second factor suggesting we were still on a journey in our pastoral care, was the strong feeling that we wanted to bring our concern for particular individuals before God in the context of the congregation's worship. Of course many congregations do this already by naming individuals in the prayers of intercession at Sunday morning worship and this approach was tried but stopped very quickly after a very unhappy experience relating to confidentiality, which made us realise that not everyone would be happy to be named in Church, especially bearing in mind the wide variety of circumstances in which people can be in hospital. Once you start to think about the issue of confidentiality you quickly begin to realise that it is quite inappropriate for any of us, either in worship or prayer group, to pray for people by name and even give details of their illness or other problems, without their specific permission to do so.

The third factor of which we became aware was that while the purpose of our pastoral care was primarily to express the love and care of God through Jesus Christ to his people, on numerous occasions the pastoral bond had brought people to worship or back to worship and to active participation in the life of the Church. This somewhat unexpected spin-off meant that we had to look more seriously at the links between pastoral care and worship.

These three factors led us over a period to identify more explicitly a number of needs which were not being met in our programme of pastoral care. These were:

1   A need to bring people and situations to God in prayer in the context of the Church's worship but without causing offence or damaging confidentiality.

2   A need to express in some symbolic but visual and even sensory way the healing, peace and wholeness that is offered by God through Jesus Christ, and to do this too in the context of the church's worship.

3   A need to have available and make use of suitable material such as Bible Readings, Prayers, Affirmations, Blessing and

Benedictions which were specifically designed to be used when a person is dying.

On the basis of these needs and over a period of several years a form of pastoral/healing worship was developed as a means of bringing to God all aspects of our caring ministry. This Service of Prayer and Blessing as its name implies contains two specific elements - an opportunity to pray for individuals by name (but only with the explicit permission of the individual concerned) and a physical expression through the giving and receiving of a blessing of the reality of the healing, peace and wholeness offered by God through Jesus Christ. Many different influences went into the preparation of this Service including attendance for a number of years at the Board of Social Responsibility's Annual Healing Conference, the Service of Healing in Common Order 1994 and Ian Cowie's book "Prayers and Ideas for Healing Services." Naturally as soon as you begin to talk about "Healing" and "Touching" some of the good folk of the Church of Scotland begin to get uneasy! Our aim in preparing the Service of Prayer and Blessing was to target a typical middle-of-the-road Church of Scotland congregation so that they would feel comfortable and at home with what was happening. You will find the full script of the Service of Prayer and Blessing in Appendix F.

As well as linking worship and pastoral care in this specific way through the Service of Prayer and Blessing, we also gathered together in an A5 display folder form a small collection of materials which we felt would be of use to us when someone was dying. Some of the prayers we produced ourselves, while other items were gathered from a range of sources. You will find details of these Readings, Prayers and Blessings for use at times when death is near in Appendix G.

There is a great need in the reformed Churches for ministers to recognise the value and importance of their pastoral role. There comes a point in terminal illness (and that happens to everyone sooner or later) when the role of the doctors and nurses is not to effect a cure because this is impossible but to make the person as comfortable as possible. It is at this time, when no further medical intervention is felt to be worthwhile that the pastoral and healing ministry of the Church is most important - in helping the individual concerned to face death and to meet God with dignity and peace, and in helping the relatives to share in the experience as fully and positively as possible, notwithstanding their inevitable grief. For that reason we need to be much less apologetic and self-effacing about what we do. We need to see that what we are able to offer through Jesus Christ is the thing that matters most at that moment and should therefore have priority over everything else.

Chapter 13

Bereavement and Pastoral Care

There must be times when even a craftsman gets fed up churning out the same old thing! In the case of a cabinet maker it is probably making the umpteenth coffee table or pair of bedside cabinets that tries his or her patience. In the case of the artist or photographer it is no doubt the family group complete with crumpled granny and snotty infant! For those of us involved in Ministrycraft the nearest equivalent is undoubtedly the funeral, simply because it is something we have to do over and over again. I have a great deal of sympathy for those who are in parishes where the number of funerals averages more than one a week, simply because this must make it very difficult to focus on other aspects of their ministry. But the frequency with which we have to conduct funeral services can open us to the danger that like the cabinet maker or the artist we get fed up with the continual slog and bored with the repetition. The reality that we can so easily miss is that taking a funeral service is a huge responsibility and a huge privilege. It is the one opportunity that the Church still has to reach those people who normally would not enter its doors, because whatever people think or feel about the Christian faith, God and religion, everyone who has any connection with the deceased person feels it is right to attend the funeral. For that one moment in time all the prejudices about the Church, all the misconceptions, and all the indifference are put aside and we are given a real opportunity to reach out and touch people when they are at their most sensitive.

But if funerals give us a unique opportunity for mission, what is much more important is that they give us a unique opportunity to express the church's pastoral care for people. At this time of grief and despair, our care and concern can be an expression of the love of God which reaches beyond death, and which can bring light into the inevitable darkness. Each funeral we conduct presents that unique moment when we, and only we, can show people that despite everything God loves them. But that can only happen if we play our part to the full. Some ministers seem to have the idea that the best way to do this is to give the gathered mourners a fifteen minute exposition of the essentials of the gospel message. For me this is the wrong thing, at the wrong place and the wrong time. I am convinced that the Gospel is preached at this time not in a one-off slot but in everything we do and say and are in relation to the funeral, from the first visit to the grieving family right through to the follow-up visit after the funeral. That makes it so important that all we do is done with sympathy, with understanding and with sensitivity. We have all heard horror stories and some of them at least must be true of mourners who have only found out later that they have attended the wrong service at the crematorium because not only was the deceased person's name never mentioned but nothing was said that was personal enough to enable them to be identified. That means simply and sadly that good ministrycraft has not been exercised and the Gospel has not been preached.

Naturally there is no "right" way to minister in the context of bereavement with the implication that all the other ways are wrong! Like so many areas of ministrycraft what you decide is best for you may be very different from your neighbour's approach or from mine. The outline that follows is therefore intended simply as a resource to help you think through your own ideas.

The First Visit

The circumstances surrounding a bereavement can be widely varied. On the one hand the deceased may be an active member of the congregation whose partner and family are well known to you. If the illness has not been sudden you will have been visiting the deceased regularly at home or in hospital and it may be the family who contact you. On the other hand the first information you receive may come through a phone call from the local undertaker asking you to conduct the funeral service. But whatever the circumstances, it is very important to make an initial visit to the principal mourner(s) as quickly as possible. It is not always possible just to drop everything and go, but not as difficult as some of us would like to make out. It is not very often that we are engaged in something that simply cannot be broken off or postponed and it would be surprising if those we are engaged with were anything but fully understanding of the circumstances. Why is this important? Put yourself in the situation and you will find the answer. Your mother has just died suddenly in the local hospital. The undertaker has been to make the arrangements for the funeral and has phoned the minister. Soon after the undertaker leaves, the minister himself, or herself arrives at the door to express his or her sympathy. Immediately a huge burden of worry and uncertainty is removed, and if the minister is a stranger, a helpful bond is formed. The alternative is that the minister phones and says, "I'll come and see you tomorrow at 11.30 am." It is not difficult to sense the difference between the two approaches and that is what makes this initial visit so crucial! Ideally it should not be to discuss the arrangements for the funeral, but simply to share in the grief and the pain that is being felt. This does not need to be a lengthy visit - what is important is being there and being there quickly! This is an opportunity to allow those most closely involved to share with you the circumstances surrounding the death. Most people have a real need to talk about all the details to someone who shows that they are genuinely interested. You may want also to invite those present to pray together. Again short is sweet and a few sentences asking God for his support in the hours and days ahead will touch what most people are probably feeling. I have found that inviting people to join hands in a circle during the prayer creates a sense of mutual support in grief that words cannot express. Some personal details can be noted at this time - full name, address, age, and details of family - and a simple form is useful for this purpose – see Appendix H. As you leave, you can enquire about a suitable day and time to call back to go over the details of the funeral arrangements. It is also helpful to say if you are happy to have suggestions for particular readings or hymns at the funeral and to indicate if you wish to put together a brief "life story" of the deceased to use as part of the service. This allows the principal mourners to think and talk about these matters before you return. A list of suggested hymns can be a good thing to leave with them, as those who are not involved in the church may want to choose hymns but not be able to remember particular favourites. This first visit can end with you leaving your card with your name, address and phone no and making it clear that you are happy to be contacted if there are any problems or questions or if there is a need to share their grief with you.

The Second Visit

This visit will focus on the details of the funeral but will begin best by inviting those present to talk about how they are feeling and how they are coping with their loss. It is likely that if you have been expected a cup of tea or coffee will be on hand and this is a good way of strengthening the pastoral relationship which is developing. Very often you may find that the immediate mourners are not familiar with what happens at a funeral and going over this can be helpful to them. For example in relation to a funeral in Church I always made a point of telling the family that when they came down the aisle to take their places in the front pew, the coffin would already be in place immediately in front of them. This is a very emotional moment at best, but if the first sight of the coffin is also unexpected it is much harder to cope with. In the same way, if the funeral is in a crematorium it is important to describe the procedures that will be followed in relation to bringing the coffin into the chapel, and what will actually happen at the moment of committal, whether it is curtains closing, dais lowering, or nothing visible. Without this information an element of shock and surprise can add greatly to the pain. It is also worth taking time to talk about the seating arrangements, and in particular to clarify where those closest to the deceased will be sitting and who will be sitting beside them. There is nothing worse than seeing a grieving husband or wife isolated at the end of a row when what they need is their son and daughter, one on each side. Going over the procedure of the funeral, will provide an opportunity to discuss any special requests that the principal mourners may have, such as particular hymns, or readings. From this point of view it is always wise to take with you on the visit a copy of the hymn book and any song books your church uses, in order to clarify what may be quite vague requests. For example a request for "the hymn we sing at christenings" needs to be clarified on the spot!

But the main purpose of this visit will be to talk about the deceased, and to gather the information you require in order to say some appropriate words at the funeral. I have always avoided using the word "eulogy" preferring to refer to it as the individual's "life story" in the hope that we can get away from making it sound as if everyone who dies is an absolute saint! But we do have to exercise considerable skill here in deciding what to say and what not to say. This is not just in relation to obvious things like indiscretions in youth or jail sentences in adulthood, but sensitive information such as marriage breakdown, illegitimate children, and particular illnesses such as cancer or aids. I have found that the best way is to ask the principal mourners themselves whether they wish a sensitive piece of information to be included. They can also be very helpful in giving you not the just the skeleton of a person's life story but the flesh and blood as well in the way of stories, memories and incidents from past years. The inclusion of such items, including humorous ones, makes the person real to those present and will no doubt bring back lots of other memories for them too. In this way, we hopefully hand over to God in the funeral service not a plaster saint, but a real person, and if that means a bit of "warts and all" so be it!

The Funeral

I have to confess right away that there are two modern trends in funerals which I personally dislike! One is the attempt to change a funeral service which is essentially a very serious event when the death of a human being is publicly acknowledged and his or her remains are committed to God, into an act of celebration with the emphasis entirely on the deceased's life rather than death. Of course a well constructed funeral service will include full recognition of all that the deceased has done, and all that his or her life has meant, and will express thanksgiving for that, but that aspect will be contained within what is and should be an occasion for solemnity and sadness. A friend (who has since died) once said to me in relation to this issue, "When it's my funeral, I want everyone to be miserable and crying, not having a celebration!" It is worth noting that when people die who are considered to be of public importance, the funeral service itself, which is often a private family affair, is often followed some weeks later by a "Service of Thanksgiving for the Life of ……… ………" and for me this makes the distinction clear.

My other personal dislike is to the practice of taking collections of money at the end of funeral services. I appreciate that the desire to support the work of a charity, particularly one that may be linked in some way to the deceased, is a worthy one, but I cannot help feeling that a funeral service is the wrong time to do this. It does seem to imply that in some way the awfulness and pain of death can be lessened if we can do something and in our society that usually means money. The truth is that no matter how much we put in the plate at the door, death is death and God is God.

Everyone who conducts funeral services will need to decide how they personally deal with these two issues, both of which arise quite regularly. In the same way, the actual content of the funeral service is very much a personal matter for the individual. There are a wide variety of resources available which will give guidance to those who are starting out, not least the Church of Scotland's 1994 Book of Common Order which has a very full section on funerals. It is only if you have found yourself in the situation of taking a funeral for a still-born child that you will appreciate as I have just how excellent that particular service is in Common Order. Old though it now is the 1967 edition of Contemporary Prayers for Public Worship edited byCaryl Micklem contains an "Order for Burial or Cremation" which has a simple fresh approach which has stood the test of time. Second hand copies may be available on the internet.

That a funeral service should contain some readings from Scripture goes without saying, and everyone has their own particular choices as well as the translations they like best of the tried and tested favourites. There is no doubt that reading a familiar lesson from a contemporary version such as "The Message" by Eugene Peterson can bring the meaning to life in a way that makes people sit up and take notice. It has also been my experience that readings from sources other than the Bible can be helpful in adding another dimension to a funeral service. All of us have no doubt been asked at one time or another to read the words of Henry Scott Holland (1847-1918) Canon of St Paul's Cathedral which begin -

"Death is nothing at all. I have only slipped away into the next room....."

Much more to my own taste, to the extent that I quote them in full in Appendix I, are the words of Deitrich Bonhoeffer in "Letters and Papers from Prison" which he wrote on Christmas Eve 1943.

The Funeral Tea

It is a natural courtesy for those most immediately involved to extend an invitation to the person conducting the funeral to whatever is taking place afterwards, which may vary from simple tea and biscuits in someone's home to a full-blown three course meal at a local hotel. There is no doubt that bereaved families feel considerable pressure to provide a suitable funeral "purvey" even if their instincts are to do nothing or something much simpler and it may be part of our role to enable them to do what they want rather than what they feel is expected. But the question of whether or not we should attend is a difficult one, and again everyone must decide for themselves. If the individual who has died and his or her family are known to you it may be entirely appropriate for you to be present. On the other hand we all take lots of funerals when we know practically no one and if we go along to the funeral tea we feel embarrassed and out-of-place and what is more are a source of discomfort to those involved. At one time or another, we have all heard the whispered instruction across the room - "Go and speak to the minister, he's all on his own." In circumstances like these it would be much better for everyone if we did not attend. There is also the question, which we shall look at in more detail later, of what is the best use of our time and of setting priorities in ministry. Hanging around at a funeral tea, particularly when through plentiful libations of alcohol some of those present turn it into a party, cannot really be top of our list of important things to do. The real problem is that, like a number of situations in ministry, if we find ourselves attending some funeral teas and not others we can put ourselves in a difficult situation and cause genuine hurt to people.

"He went to that woman's 'do', and she was never near the church, but when Uncle Willie died he said he was too busy."

One way round this, which I myself employed, was simply to gently but firmly refuse all invitations to funeral teas, except in very special circumstances where an exception could not be misunderstood. There were times when it was not entirely easy to stick to this rule, but by and large it seemed to work satisfactorily. Most people will understand that it is not necessarily the best use of your time, and many people will be secretly relieved that they do not have to cope with your presence, and can relax with their family and friends. One word of warning - if you are working in a team situation with an associate, assistant, probationer or pastoral assistant, you do need to agree your policy on this together and stick to it - there is nothing more divisive in a congregation than comparisons being made about things like this. "Isn't it nice that the assistant minister came to the funeral tea. Why can't the minister do that as well?"

The Third Visit

Once the funeral is over, we have an opportunity to express real care by making a further visit to those most closely involved. This visit has no practical function in the sense that there is nothing to be done, but going to the door a day or two after the funeral to ask how people are, to give them the chance to talk about the funeral, and to share again in their grief, is an expression of genuine care which it is difficult to over-state. Simply because in a sense there is no real need for this visit, it is clearly seen to be exactly what it is - the church showing care for people in their need. Of course every minister agrees in principle with what I have said but feels they are far too busy for this "post-funeral visit" as I call it. I would like to suggest that the value of this particular visit is so high, the impact it may have is so great, and the opportunities it may open up are so important, that we need to give it a very high rating when we decide our priorities for our ministry. For example, it is sometimes at this "post-funeral visit" that the conversation can take you from the funeral service itself to questions of personal faith and belief. It has happened at this visit that a person has decided that they would really like to start attending church again - and do so! This visit may bring up ways in which the church can offer ongoing help or support, for example by undertaking further visits to a bereaved individual, or by inviting him or her to join a bereavement support group.

Follow Up to Bereavement

There are various ways in which the church can follow up on its care of those who have been bereaved. A bereavement support group is one way of doing this, and this provides the opportunity for people who are suffering in the same way to share and talk about their feelings and the difficulties they are having. Some individuals may be so damaged by bereavement, that regular visits from the pastoral team over a period of weeks or even months are desirable. If you are operating the idea of a gift of flowers or a plant at Easter or Harvest Thanksgiving, it is not difficult to include on the list all those who have been bereaved during the last year, and this is a good way of letting people know that they have not been forgotten. Some churches have introduced a special annual memorial service, often on or around All Saints Day, to which bereaved relatives are specially invited.

As I said at the beginning of this chapter, "each funeral we conduct provides that unique moment when we can show people that despite everything God loves them." I hope that what I have said has made it clear that this is true not just of the funeral service itself, but of everything that we do surrounding it.

Chapter 14

Communication is King!

It doesn't seem all that long ago when the biggest worry when your car broke down was finding a phone to call the AA and one of their biggest roles along with the RAC was to provide phone boxes in remote places. Now you use your mobile! It doesn't seem all that long ago when the biggest worry when one of your family went abroad on holiday was how they would manage to get in touch to let you know they had arrived safely. Now they send you a text message! There is no doubt that as we move into the twenty first century communication is king. It is difficult to absorb just how quickly and how much the technology has changed not just in a lifetime, but in a few years, and the one thing that is sure is that it will go on changing. It is changing the way we live and the way we think, as we adjust to viewing our telephone bills and paying them online, doing all our banking from the comfort of our homes, and shopping for everything from holidays to new cars and even houses on the internet. On retiral we purchased a house in a new estate and found that several of our new neighbours had signed up for their houses on the internet without having seen the site or the show house.

So how is the church handling all this? How well is it surviving in a world in which communication is king? The answer is not very well! In fact so bad is the church at communicating that it is to a large extent not even using effectively the old, traditional, pre-electronic methods, far less the new, cool, twenty first century methods. Of course like all sweeping generalisations, that one can be proved wrong, so perhaps the best thing is to look at some of the specific means of communication the church uses and ministers use so that we can ask ourselves how well we are doing in our particular situation.

The Intimations

If I have one pet hate in the whole of the church it is the word "Intimations!" It seems to reek of the very worst of middle-class victorian attitudes, where so much to do with church seemed to need special, posh words to describe it. No one ever talks about "Intimations" in normal life, and yet we go on happily using the word and accepting it just because we are inside the building. I can still hear my childhood minister intoning in his best pulpit voice, "Here are the Intimations!" What's wrong with "Announcements?" That's what they are and that's what they should be called and I challenge everyone in the church who uses the word "Intimations" to justify why they are doing so. Can it really be as one minister's wife from the borders said to me, "It's aye bin that!" Having got that off my chest, there is a place today for Announcements as part of the Service, so long as we realise their limitations. Do we seriously expect anyone to absorb and remember a whole week of church events, including times places and even phone numbers as they are rattled off from the pulpit? And inevitably the more there are, the more they are rattled! The Announcements should never be just announced. But they can be useful to *back up* announcements that are already included in print in a weekly worship leaflet which is presumably put into the hands of worshippers at the door and also includes details of the order of service. "Can I draw your attention to Announcement 6 in the Worship Leaflet - I hope everyone will do their best to attend the Stated Annual Meeting this Wednesday evening" seems to me to be a good way of using Announcements effectively but briefly. By and large the church has failed to realise that people are just not able to retain a lot of spoken information. Just think how long some ministers preach! Of course there are situations where something will have to be announced at the last minute, for example the day and time of the funeral of a member of the congregation, and the impact and importance of this announcement will be enhanced if it is one of only a few that are given verbally.

The Worship Leaflet

I appreciate that for some readers a weekly worship leaflet will not be something you are familiar with, but perhaps you should be! One of the great things about the technological revolution is that it has become so quick and easy and inexpensive to produce something like a worship leaflet - one sheet of A4 paper folded in half is enough - that even if the minister has to do it himself or herself there is really no excuse for not having one. The front page can be devoted to the order of service for that Sunday morning, which leaves two inside pages and the back which can be used for additional worship material, eg the words of a song, or filled completely with announcements. Of course many churches are now producing much more sophisticated worship leaflets with attractive graphics on the front cover and several pages devoted to the order of service and announcements, still leaving space perhaps for daily devotional material for the week or news of community as well as church events. There must be very few congregations where someone cannot be cajoled into being the church printer, spending a few hours each week putting together the worship leaflet preferably using suitable DTP software. As far as running off copies of the original is concerned, the modern equivalent of the old-fashioned turn-the-handle duplicator may be expensive to purchase, but once you have done so the cost per copy is little more than the paper and because it scans electronically it will cope with graphics as well as printing. I would go so far as to suggest that the purchase of such a machine can change a church, because it makes it easy and cheap to make the communication work well.

One of the biggest advantages of a weekly worship leaflet comes as a spin off - there has to be a deadline for all the material so that the printer can go to work! That is good for the minister, because it means that decisions about the order of service such as the choice of praise and the scripture readings have to be made in time to meet the deadline whether it is Thursday at noon or Friday at 9 am or whenever. That is a good discipline for the minister because it means that at least some thought has to be given relatively early in the week to the theme for the service and the sermon, and makes it impossible to leave everything until Saturday night. It is also good for the congregation because it means that those who are actively involved in groups and organisations have to make their announcements available to meet the weekly deadline and thankfully brings to an end the practice of rushing into the Vestry at two minutes to eleven and pressing a scribbled note on a page torn from a school jotter into the minister's hand. Well organised and well presented the weekly printed announcements can be a useful communication tool in the congregation because of their immediacy. The one obvious drawback which we always need to keep in mind is that they only reach those who are present at worship, that is in most congregations about one third of the membership. So don't be tempted into thinking that if you put an event in the weekly worship leaflet the whole church knows about it - they don't!

The Church Magazine

If you ask people in the Church about how they communicate, most would mention first of all the church magazine. In fact they might not even think of "The Intimations" or the Worship Leaflet at all! Obviously there are huge variations in the style and content of church magazines, depending largely on the resources of the congregation both in terms of finance and people. If you have an enthusiastic member who is employed in IT and enjoys playing around with DTP in his or her spare time, then you are quids in and your magazine is likely to be well presented and produced. Cost is not nearly as important a factor as it used to be, as today's technology has made it unnecessary to engage the services of a professional printer.

(By the way if you want to be cool and *with it* in ministry, it is very important that you know what all these abbreviations mean. IT = Information Technology and DTP = Desk Top Publishing. You also need to be ready to answer questions such as - "What kind of CPU (Central Processing Unit) have you?" and "What size is your hard disk?")

The arrangements for the production and distribution of church magazines tend to continue along the same lines year after year after year unless some far-sighted person starts asking some probing questions. If you want to take a fresh look at what you are doing, try these for starters!

1 If your church magazine is only produced once every three months, ask yourself if it is fulfilling any real purpose in communicating to the congregation. It is very difficult to look that far ahead with sufficient detail for it to be useful, and accounts of past events become very far in the past. If not, then does it have another useful role which makes it worth continuing, for example as a kind of local version of Life and Work? If not, is it worth doing at all?

2 Assuming your church magazine is produced every month, is it reaching the people you want it to reach? It seems fairly obvious that the magazine needs to go into the home of every member of

the congregation, but if you only get the magazine if you pay a subscription, then that will not happen.

3   Are the delivery arrangements effective? No matter how good a magazine is, if all we do is put a pile in the church porch and invite people to help themselves, then it cannot be a good communication tool. Many churches have a team of magazine deliverers and this is an excellent way of ensuring that the magazine reaches everyone, though there is still an important task to do in keeping lists of names and addresses up-to-date. New members of the congregation are the very ones you want to be sure get their copy immediately they join.

4   Should the church magazine be more widely distributed? In many communities today there is a distinct lack of social contact and community spirit, and a church magazine which contains not just church news but news about what is going on in the community as a whole can be an important means of developing some sense of community as well as putting the church on the map. That assumes of course that the magazine will go into every home in the parish or community and that may be a huge task that is quite beyond the resources of a congregation. However there can be a middle way, where the church magazine is delivered to every member, but also circulated widely in the community through library, school, health centre, dentist's waiting room, and shops. It also means that news about what the Church is doing is reaching a wider audience - and you never know what effect that might have!

Naturally the content of church magazines varies just as much as their layout. Much can be done to make a magazine look attractive and readable through good use of DTP, but if the content consists of nothing but long, boring articles about the Westminster Confession most people are going to be switched off. A quick look at the popular press will make us realise that short, snappy articles which catch the attention are the way to communicate today. Graphics and illustrations can help a great deal as long as the quality is reasonable, but it is better not to use them than publish a half page of black and grey fuzz which is supposed to be the minister at the Sunday School picnic - if you still have one! A good rule of thumb in looking at the content of your church magazine is to assume that the person who is reading it knows nothing about the church. In practice this may not be too far from the truth in the sense that the majority of the members are non-attenders and inevitably out-of-touch with what is happening. I am often surprised that church magazines do not begin with what I think is the most important information of all - details about the services of worship. In fact I have seen magazines where there is no mention of worship - either they don't do it or they assume that everyone knows it is at ll am every Sunday. Details of the worship should be the biggest thing in every church magazine, and in particular those congregations where there are variations in times or places from one Sunday to another, or different types of Service on different Sundays. That is the kind of information that people go to the Church Magazine for, and it needs to be there every month. Never assume that everyone knows - they will have forgotten! I have heard ministers saying - "I have introduced a Vestry Hour but no one ever comes - they still come to the door or phone me up at 10 o'clock at night." The first question to ask is – Have you told them there is a Vestry Hour? Are you continuing to tell them there is a Vestry Hour? Does it feature *every* Sunday in the announcements and in the worship leaflet and is it mentioned *every* month in the church magazine? Do these announcements not only say where and when the Vestry Hour takes place, but what its purpose is? The doorbell rings - "Could you sign my passport form please? I didn't come to Vestry Hour because I thought that was for people with problems."

Apart from information about worship, the church magazine provides endless opportunities to communicate with the congregation

- not just to give them information, but to seek their support and to give them encouragement. It is impossible to cover all the possibilities of material that can be included but I would suggest three possible rules of thumb:

1 Try to ensure that the magazine overall has a positive and encouraging feel to it. It is very easy in these times of falling membership and financial difficulties for the church magazine to be devoted exclusively to requests for more money and raps over the knuckles for non-attendance. Neither of these approaches is likely to work, but it also means that the magazine as a whole gives off very negative vibes.

2 In the same way it is important that the magazine does not come across as being exclusively for those who are actively involved in the church's life and make those who are on the fringe feel either unwanted or even guilty. We all know that the church's first mission today is not to Africa but we have not entirely taken on board that neither is it to the great unchurched of our land. It is first of all to that huge group of people who are on the rolls of churches throughout Scotland but who are effectively no longer part of the community of faith in any real sense.

3 A good church magazine will encourage a congregation to lift their heads and look beyond their own patch. Of course we all know that Life and Work exists to do just that, but how many of our members read it? We need to do our bit to let people know that the Church is bigger (and maybe better) than they think and that exciting and positive things are happening both in Scotland and around the world.

The Press

Most newspapers run a column of adverts for church services. No doubt it was a hangover from our past when Scotland was ostensibly

Christian that this was done free of charge, but this is no longer the case. The result is that most churches have decided that the expense is too great and have stopped submitting their adverts with the result that the "Church Notices" column in most papers is occupied only by other denominations and religious groups. This seems a pity as it gives the wrong impression to anyone reading the paper. If you are a visitor to Stirling for example (and there are lots of them and some of them must want to go to church) you would get the impression from the Stirling Observer that the only functioning Christian groups in the area are the Destiny Church and the Dunblane Free Church. Maybe we need to think again about this, and at least make full enquiry as to the actual cost. It may not be as expensive as we think!

Apart from paid adverts most local newspapers run a page with news from around the area which they serve, and are usually only too glad to have input from the churches. This is a tremendous opportunity as it is in effect advertising for free, which makes it surprising that so many churches do not take advantage of it, or else submit material that is of little interest to readers. A quick read at the rest of the paper will make it obvious that it is news about people that makes local communities tick. "The Sacrament of Baptism was celebrated last Sunday in St Andrew's Church" is hardly worth printing but "Emma Brown, infant daughter of Jim and Susan of Upper Smith Street let out a squeal of delight when she was baptised by the Rev John Brown in St Andrew's Church last Sunday, then burst into tears!" is much more interesting. Keeping a regular column going every week in the local paper is hard work, but does not have to be done by the minister. If you have the manpower a Church Press Officer is an excellent appointment for the right person who may well develop the role into local radio as well as the newspapers.

In thinking about communication in general but in particular the press, there are three things we have to remember. One is that this is a form of outreach into the community, making people aware that the church does exist and from this point of view the impression that we make is very important. The second is that people like to read about themselves and their church, and regular coverage creates a "feel good" factor for the members themselves which should not be underestimated. The third is that for those members of the congregation who are unable to attend church because of age or illness, regular news in the local papers helps to keep them in touch and makes them feel they are still part of things. Here are two extracts from the "District Digest" of the same local paper which seem to support some of the above points.

St John's Church

On Sunday at the morning service, Mr John Smith was the guest preacher. He brought some thoughts on the Letter of James. The Evening Service........

(Riveting stuff isn't it! Makes you wish you had been there!)

Boys' Brigade

On Saturday evening four boys travelled to Wishaw to take part in the semi-final stages of Masterteams. The boys finished in third place. Those representing the company were Alastair Dougall, Iain Sinclair, Malcolm Duncan, and Scott Ferguson.

("Mum, my name's in the paper!")

The Notice Board

There is one other communication resource available to us, that is so traditional that we often forget about it, and that is the Church Notice Board. Situated outside the Church, it is in an ideal position to communicate with those who are passing or have come specially, but usually it tells us very little beyond the name of the Church and the name of the minister, though sometimes the name and address of the session clerk is included for some obscure reason. Usually some attempt is made to give details of the service or services of worship though that is not always easy to understand and may not even be accurate, particularly in complex linkages. It is often so long since the Notice Board was given any attention that at worst it is difficult to read and at best gives an impression of being caught in a time warp. It is not something that churches on the whole give a very high priority to, as is made clear when the minister changes, and a sign writer is engaged not to renew the whole Notice Board but simply to delete the name of the last incumbent by overpainting the new one. Just ask yourself what kind of impression that gives to passers by! That is probably one of the most important things about a Notice Board, that apart from imparting information, it gives an impression of the church from the outside. What chance is there of anyone coming into the church if the message out in the street is that we are tired, dull and not that bothered?

It is possible for a Notice Board to be very different from that, but you have to work at it. In the first place it must be in good condition, fresh and bright. Secondly it must tell people what they want to know and that includes the following:

What is the name of this Church?
What denomination does it belong to?
Who is the minister?
When are the services of worship?
How can I get in touch?

One way of doing this very effectively is to have a Notice Board with two panels - one with fixed information which does not need to be changed, and one where fresh information can be inserted every week. If you think that all your information is fixed because your worship is always at 11 am every Sunday of the year, stop and think a bit more! A visitor to your town or community will want to know if he or she is going to arrive at church only to discover it is Communion. If you live in a city or tourist area, visitors over the christmas period may well be looking for a church where there is a Watchnight Service. That kind of information needs to go on the Notice Board and needs to be updated every week. This can be another job for your new Press Officer - just rename him or her as Press and Communication Manager! Or if you have a Church Secretary, one of the first tasks for a Monday morning can be to change the Church Notice Board. If you have the resources, then the ideal is a Notice Board with three panels, the centre one with fixed information, one side for weekly worship information and the other side for that poster you have had pressed into your hands for the Guide Coffee Morning or the Guild Outing. Of course a good Notice Board like this, strong enough to withstand the vagaries of the weather and threats of vandalism does not come cheap. If you can't persuade your Congregational Board to part with the money, put it on the list you keep of projects that are suitable for consideration when you are approached regarding a bequest or memorial gift to the church – you may find that a new and attractive Notice Board outside the Church can be seen as an attractive alternative to a lectern or pew cushions.

When we are thinking about Notice Boards, it is worth noting that the Church often communicates, mostly to its members, through a Notice Board or series of Notice Boards inside the church premises which are used to display everything from posters for Life and Work to appeals for volunteers to lead the Brownies. Once again, the impression that this gives is important, and if posters remain on the Notice Board months after the event until they are torn and tired, then it is not just a waste of valuable space on the Notice Board, it is sending out all the wrong messages. The best way of dealing with this is to have someone in charge of the Notice Board(s) who is responsible for putting up items before the event and for removing them afterwards. It may be worth bearing in mind that some of the people who pass your Notice Board have no connection with the church - parents bringing their kids to Jumping Beans or collecting their boys from Cubs. So maybe some information about the Church and its worship is worth putting up, as well as details about the minister's Vestry Hour in case someone wants to talk.

The Internet

Many Churches are beginning to take advantage of the new technology and are setting up websites on the internet. Like church magazines these vary hugely in quality, depending largely on the human and financial resources the congregation has available. Of course the ideal is to go to a company whose business is setting up websites and have it done professionally, but there is no reason why it cannot be done effectively by someone in the congregation who is in this line of work or who is an enthusiastic amateur. The most important thing in setting up a website is to make it clear and simple to use, bearing in mind that many of those whom you wish to access it will not be all that familiar with computers or comfortable on the internet. If it looks good as well so much the better. The best way to start is to look at what other people have done. This will give you lots of ideas about what you want (and don't want!) to do yourself. The Church of Scotland website (www.churchofscotland.org.uk) has a Directory of Churches with websites (from the Home Page go to "Contact Us") and browsing through these is very illuminating. The exciting thing about the internet is its immediacy - information can be put on your website and is available immediately to anyone who wants to look at it. Think of it as an electronic church notice board with a constantly changing and widely varied range of material and you begin to get the idea. For that reason it seems to me there is little point in setting up a website which is nothing more than a nice picture of the church and the name, address and phone number of the minister so that it never changes from week to week or month to month. Someone accessing your website should be able to find out quickly and easily exactly what is happening in your church today, tomorrow, next Sunday, and next week. Looking at different websites it is surprising to see that the most important information about the services of worship is not the first thing that is available but often has to be ferreted out from a lot of other details. Surprising too to note how many churches open their websites with information about their church building, as if that was the most important thing they wanted to communicate.

But *the* most important thing about a church website, is that it *must* be kept up-to-date! There is absolutely no point in going to a lot of expense and/or time in setting up a site, if it is not constantly updated. That means every week at the very least, and ideally more often. If I am a member at St Bride's and hear that a member of the congregation has died, I want to be able to access the website and get the details of the arrangements for the funeral service. That means having a good website is hard work. Like other tasks in communication it is best if someone other than the minister can undertake this ongoing task, though the minister still has a crucial role to play in constantly passing on information. To be perfectly frank some of the church websites I have looked at are doing more harm than good. As far as members of the congregation are concerned the information is all out of date, and as far as interested outsiders are concerned "We're not going there – they're still showing their Christmas Services and it's the middle of February!"

The other very important thing to remember about a website is that not everyone has a computer and not everyone wants to go online, so we cannot assume that if we put some information on our site it has reached everyone. In fact that is what makes the whole business of communicating in the church interesting and uncertain, that there is no one way that will guarantee you access to everyone. Probably the single most effective method is still the monthly church magazine, but we are entirely dependent on people sitting down and reading it once we have put it through their letter boxes and experience has shown that this does not always happen. That means the best answer is "a bit of everything!" Use all the means of communication we have looked at in this chapter that are available to you as best you can and others too. Some of it will work, at least some of the time!

Church Postman

There is one other means of communicating in the church that is worth looking at. A congregation that is actively involving its members in different aspects of church life will need to communicate with them on a regular basis. Rotas for offering duties, welcome at the door, delivery of flowers, and all sorts of other things can be published in the church magazine or go on the website. A full directory of members' email addresses can make communication between the church and some of its members quick and easy. But if weekly reminders to those on duty at the church door, creche, coffee, etc need to be sent out, it is worth considering having a Church Postman, assuming your congregational area is reasonably compact. If it is your turn as the Church Postman you turn up at the Manse or the Church Office on a Wednesday morning (or whenever suits in the local situation) collect all the items that are waiting and deliver them through the doors. Just as important as the saving in the cost of postage is the saving in time and the knowledge that the reminders for Sunday have reached the people concerned on time. Of course the Church Postman can be used to deliver a wide variety of other church mail and it is another way in which people who may feel they have little to offer in service to the church can be involved.

Chapter 15

What kind of minister?

Do you want to be a "crafty" minister? Doesn't sound good does it, but if all we have said so far about the "craft" of ministry has some truth in it then there could be worse things than being the kind of minister who uses all of his or her skills and develops all of his or her gifts through training and experience in the service of Jesus Christ and his Church. It also raises the question "What kind of minister do I want to be?" and sooner or later every minister has to make up his or her mind about that. It may take some time before that realisation dawns, because all of us set out in ministry with either some pretty definite ideas about it or else with a "wait and see where it takes us" attitude. If we are in the first category - "I know what kind of minister I am going to be" - the realities of actually doing the job for six months or a year make us realise in most cases that our preconceptions are totally inadequate. If we are in the second category - "I'll wait and see where it takes me" - we soon realise that you cannot sit on the fence and if we do not make up our minds the job will do it for us. So what kind of minister do you want to be? Naturally we reply - "What's the choice?" If you don't recognise the following minister-types have a look at yourself or at the ministers you know round about you. If they all seem the same to you, you are not looking carefully enough!

Choice 1   The *I want to be nice and liked by everyone* minister

Naturally we all want to be in this category.   No one wants confrontation, trouble, or bad feeling in a congregation.   But we also have to recognise that the price of constant and total popularity is that we always agree with everyone, never suggest that anything is less than wonderful, and are prepared to put our own thoughts and feelings aside on a permanent basis.   That does not sound particularly healthy either for the minister or the congregation, but there are situations where it seems to work very well.

Choice 2   The *I want to get my own way at all times* minister

This sounds at first like the opposite of Choice 1 as it will inevitably lead to conflict.   But that is not always the case, as there are congregations who respond to a very authoritative style of ministry and seem happy to accept that 'what the minister says, goes.'   Its weakness lies in the lack of active participation by the members which means in turn that they do not grow.

Choice 3   The *All things to all people* minister

In every congregation there is bound to be a wide variety of people with different outlooks and different ideas about everything from politics to women elders.   There are some ministers who try very hard to get alongside everyone.   If they like jazz, you like jazz.   If they prefer to holiday in Arran, you love Lochranza.   If they are into body piercing, you have a ring in your nose!   Well, maybe not as far as that, but I am sure you get the drift.   The trouble with this is that the minister finishes up being some kind of chameleon and sooner or later he or she will get himself or herself all tangled up.   "She told me she hates canelloni.   How come she told you she loves it?"   Not only that but the minister really becomes a non-person, nothing more than a reflection, and that is not good.

Choice 4   The *I'm very holy* minister

There's nothing wrong with holy, as long as it doesn't mean that people cannot talk to you in a normal way about normal things. If you find yourself quoting a text from Revelation in the middle of a discussion about the relative merits of Toyota and Vauxhall cars then you are definitely in danger of falling into this category. The problem with this kind of minister is that while a small number of folk may respond, the vast majority of the ordinary punters will be turned off, simply because it is somehow just what they expect a minister to be like. Holy is great, but in small doses please.

Choice 5   The *I'm hip man* minister

Everything from the way this minister dresses to the way he or she speaks gives out the same very strong message - "You may be old and fuddy-duddy and so may the Church but I am definitely hip and trendy." This apparently means it is OK to wear an old khaki army great coat on hospital visits or a mini skirt and fish net tights at communion! Seriously, there is nothing wrong with being *hip* if that is the way you really are. So long as everyone understands where you are coming from and it does not create barriers between you and a chunk of your congregation.

That is just five examples of minister types and I have no doubt that now we have got going you could add lots more to the list. If that is all a bit of fun it does raise again the very serious question with which we began the chapter - What kind of minister do *you* want to be? In the end there can only really be one answer and it comes in two parts - "Try to be yourself" and 'Try to obey these familiar words of Jesus – "Follow me."' If you are into original sin, then these two things are in a sense contradictory, but I am firmly convinced that they go together as well. Really "being yourself" - being honest about who you are and trying to be true to the best that is within you rather than playing games with yourself and other people - seems to me to be making a good start in trying to follow Jesus. If you can manage that at all there is no doubt that two things will happen. First of all you will keep your sanity in a very difficult and demanding job, because that is what ministry is. Being true to yourself means saying sometimes, "I don't know" rather than feeling you have to come up with an answer. Being true to yourself means saying sometimes, "I'm tired" rather than flogging yourself to death. Being true to yourself means crying when you feel like crying and laughing when you feel like laughing. The other thing that will happen is that if you can manage to be yourself rather than someone else - no more putting on acts thinking that that will impress people or make them like you more - then people will come to like *you* and respect *you.* That will happen, not because you are perfect, not because you are very holy, not because you agree with them all the time, but because they recognise you as another human being just like them, but a human being with some kind of integrity, and a human being who like them is trying to follow Jesus.

When I listen to people talking about their ministers, or nomination committees talking about the kind of minister their church needs, I recognise two very familiar models - Leader and Enabler. It is easy to caricature these two models by saying that in a church with a leader he or she makes everything happen, while in a church with an enabler he or she makes nothing happen! Many people will associate the Leader model with a more traditional style of ministry where the minister seemed to do everything and the role of the congregation was at best to get behind him or her as a back-up. In the same way many will associate the Enabler model with a more modern style of ministry where the minister tries to get behind the congregation and "enable" them (or even push them!) into more positive roles. To take one example, the "Leader" minister would be disinclined to allow members of the congregation to lead worship, while the "Enabler" would do everything possible to encourage them.

In fact most ministers today have a bit of both the Leader and the Enabler, and that seems to me to be a very healthy approach. We certainly want to move on from the extreme Leader style of ministry where the minister called all the shots and made all the decisions and the congregation acted as a kind of audience and not much more. Thank goodness we are discovering that the church is much more than that - nothing less than the people of God - and that being the church means enabling everyone to develop their ministry of love and service whether that means preaching the sermon or making the tea or helping those in trouble. But as always in situations of change there is a risk of throwing out the baby with the bath water, and we can go so completely overboard on the "enabling" ministry that we lose something valuable. There are times when a church needs a "Leader" minister. From experience I would suggest that one of these times is when there is trouble in the congregation, possibly between individuals or groups and the "Leader" is needed to negotiate a peace treaty or even bang heads together! Another of these times is when a congregation is in mourning for one reason or another and needs the "Leader" to give expression to their pain. But most important of all, every church needs the kind of leader vision that comes from their minister preaching regularly to them. It is in that way that the church will continue to discover how to be the church - by seeing the vision of the leader and by grasping it, accepting it, questioning it, even rejecting it. That means it is really tough being the kind of minister who is strong enough to be both Leader and Enabler, but more than that strong enough to accept that even the vision we offer as Leader enables the church to find its own vision which may not necessarily be ours. Yes, it is tough being a minister, but of course no one said it was going to be easy.

Chapter 16

Sharing Ministry

There is no doubt that the traditional pattern of ministry in the Church of Scotland is fast disappearing. No longer can we assume that "one minister to one congregation" is the norm and anything else is the exception. There are many ministers serving today who will have known only linked charges throughout their ministry. The current major shortage of ministers is increasing the pressure to spread ministers more thinly on the ground and various structures are being developed along these lines. But even if that was not happening the trend seems to be away from the "isolationist" concept of ministry towards a more cooperative shared approach involving ministers in working much more with each other and with the members of their congregations. For years we have paid lip service to the "priesthood of all believers" within our Presbyterian tradition but now it is fast becoming a reality bringing with it the need for radical changes in attitude on all sides. Practising ministry in this new environment is going to be very different from what it was. It will demand new skills of ministers and at the same time present new and exciting opportunities.

The Board of National Mission in its report to the 2002 General Assembly made this comment on ministers working together in team ministry - "..... there is usually too much theological and personality baggage to be able to form a true team situation. It makes greater sense to appoint team leaders, and allow them, in conjunction with others, to build up a team...." That is a pretty powerful condemnation of the attitudes of ministers and makes it abundantly clear just how big a change there needs to be. First this whole business of whether you are conservative or liberal theologically has to stop being a barrier that makes it impossible for people to pull together effectively. Second, ministers have to stop being prima donnas who are so set in their ways that they cannot work with others. The Board of National Mission was undoubtedly right in its conclusion that the best way to approach this is by appointing team leaders who build a team around them, but it is an admission of failure - that ministers cannot or will not function satisfactorily in a team situation where they are equally sharing everything. If these attitudes are to change it will require effort at every level, but particularly in training for ministry and especially in placements both as candidates and probationers. If future ministers can see existing ministers working well together whether in teams or other forms of cooperation, that will have a far greater impact than any amount of lectures or conference discussions.

Unfortunately most of the cooperation that goes on between congregations and ministers is still at a fairly minimal level. Whether within the Church of Scotland or along with other denominations it tends to be of the "sharing services in Holy Week" variety and as hardly anybody goes to these anyway the impact is virtually non existent. It seems a pity that efforts at cooperation seem to focus on special occasions like Christmas, Easter, Christian Aid Week or the Week of Prayer for Christian Unity, rather than attempting to share together at "normal" times and on "ordinary" occasions. Maybe we need to recognise that one of the most difficult things to do is to share worship particularly across denominations. It is very easy to talk about holding a "United Service" but actually doing it is fraught with difficulties. Even the question of where to hold it creates problems and may influence who attends. And that is only the beginning, because the next question is what form the service will take. Stalwart members of the Church of Scotland can easily be put off turning out during Holy Week if the service each evening follows the form for "Compline" in the Scottish Episcopal Church. Equally Episcopal members may find a Church of Scotland "hymn sandwich" not to their taste! On top of that we have to ask ourselves how much has been achieved if all we have done is given people the opportunity to attend a Church of Scotland or Episcopal Service in the guise of being "united." The real challenge is to devise an expression of Christian worship that is not tied to the liturgical traditions of any one denomination. That is extremely demanding both in terms of time and of the levels of sharing and cooperating between ministers that we talked about earlier.

Another possibility is to avoid the major difficulties of "united" worship and look at other areas in which congregations and ministers can usefully work together. Bible Study Groups which cross parish and denominational boundaries are happening in some areas, as are classes in preparation for church membership with the obvious advantages of bigger numbers and a wider vision of the nature of the church. But that is only a start and initiatives like "Church without Walls" are slowly but surely beginning to have an impact. There are some exciting things happening and there is no doubt that we are beginning to realise that we *can* think "out of the box" about ministry. The Church of Scotland's Ministries Council produced a report for the General Assembly of 2009 entitled "Enabling Ministries – A Review of Theological Foundations for Training" which I personally found exciting and even inspiring – not something we can always say about General Assembly reports. It laid down some core principles for Enabling Ministries which are relevant far beyond the specifics of training and for that reason worth repeating –

Enjoying Community
Choosing to be Together
Connecting Context and Gospel
Enabling Maturity
Supporting Change
Swimming against the Tide – Being Prophetic
Giving of our Best – Relying on Grace
Drawing on Experiences

If these headings do not mean very much that is because you have not read this report – do so now! You will find it in the extranet area of the Church of Scotland website – www.churchofscotland.org.uk - under General Assembly Archives. But don't just read it, accept the invitation contained in it to further discussion and debate.

Chapter 17

O & M - Meetings
and
More Meetings

One of the cliches that people churn out about the church is that "It's a business like any other business." It usually arises when the discussion has got round to problems about money and someone is advocating annual subscriptions for members of the church just like the Golf Club. The truth is that the Church is certainly not a business like any other business. In fact it couldn't be more different from a business if it tried because the purpose of most businesses is to make money by selling a product or a service, while the purpose of the Church is to change the world! But if we are ever going to do that we need to use all the tools that are at our command, and one of these tools is to be efficient, organised and business-like in the way we go about things. A cabinet maker may produce the most beautiful and well-made furniture you can hope for, but unless he gives close attention to the financial and sales side of his business as well as the actual production he is doomed to failure. For some reason which I do not fully understand the Church almost seems to pride itself on being worse than useless when it comes to O & M (Organisation and Management) as if there was some some kind of virtue to be gained from shambling chaos. The other side of the coin also seems to be true for reasons which I also do not understand, that ministers and congregations who do a good job of their O & M are looked on with some suspicion as having sold out to the secular world. I want to make it quite clear that while I am one hundred per cent committed to the uniqueness of the Church and its purpose, I am also one hundred per cent committed to using all the tools and skills of O & M to enable the Church to fulfil its unique purpose as effectively as possible.

There are five areas of O & M which we are going to explore in this chapter and the following four – Meetings and More Meetings; Sub Committees Teams and Working Groups; The Church Secretary and the Church Office; Making It All Work; and The Church as Employer.

Meetings and More Meetings

The church is at work in all sorts of ways. When the church worships it is at its work. When the church gives pastoral support it is at its work. But when it comes to making decisions, deciding policy, planning events, thinking about the future, the Church works mainly through meetings and minutes and agendas and working groups and teams and committees. Go into 121 George Street, which houses most of the offices of the Church of Scotland, and look at the daily indicator board and you will see what I mean - a continual succession of meetings on a wide variety of topics with a vast selection of people involved. Go along to your local Presbytery and you will find the same thing - the mainstay of the Presbytery is a monthly meeting which deals with a wide range of items relating to the churches "within its bounds" as it is rather quaintly put. The General Assembly is unique in lots of ways but when you think about it, it is just a very long meeting with a very long Agenda. Whether that is the way the Church should work is a huge question - maybe we should spend the time praying or celebrating rather than meeting - but it is not one that I am going to pursue at the moment. What I do want to pursue is some ways of making the existing system work as well as possible.

There is no doubt that when it comes to meetings as the saying goes "the devil is in the detail." (Strangely enough that expression probably began its life as "God is in the details" and is attributed to the French novelist Gustave Flaubert.) Anyway, whether it is God or the devil the meaning is clear that small things are really important if you want a meeting to be effective. Put a dozen people in a dusty, damp, dimly lit and poorly heated room and it is very unlikely that you will start a revolution in the church! The surroundings matter and so does the seating - if you really want people to participate and contribute don't sit them in rows facing a table at the front - try a circle or a horse-shoe so that everyone can see everyone else and the person in the chair is not so dominant. But even before the meeting there are details that have to be attended to. There is no use expecting people to agree to some new venture if you present it to them on a plate without any forewarning. They will suspect that they are being steam-rollered and they are probably right! So if there is a big issue that you want your Kirk Session to look at, draft a paper beforehand and circulate it to them all. Or be prepared to have a discussion about it and then postpone a final decision until the next meeting. That way everyone gets a chance to think about it, and the jungle drums will reach those who were not present so that if they have strong views they can come along.

When it comes to routine meetings, the most important thing to do before the meeting is to prepare an Agenda. Run off copies on your duplicator or copier and everyone can have one. This way, everyone knows exactly what is going on, and there is less chance of wandering down blind alleys. A sample Agenda for a Kirk Session meeting (Unitary Constitution) is attached as Appendix J. One of the first items on the Agenda will be to approve the Minutes of the last meeting. The ideal way to deal with this is for the Minutes to be printed, copied and circulated, so that everyone has a chance to read them beforehand. There is nothing gets a meeting off to a bad start in terms of sheer dullness, than having to sit through the reading by the Clerk of a hand-written Minute. It is a useful idea to have an item at the beginning of the Agenda called "Order of Business" which means that the Agenda as it is printed is agreed or amended and anyone who wants to bring something else up has to indicate this at the beginning of the meeting. It is much better to know at 7.40 pm that Mrs Brown wants to talk about the state of the tea urns in the church kitchen and to add it to the Agenda under "Fabric" than to have it sprung on you at ten minutes to ten when you and everyone else is thinking, "I'll maybe get home in time to see the news." Having done that at the beginning of the meeting the Agenda is effectively "closed" and no new items can be added. Even better is to have a deadline for items for the Agenda which is 24 hours or even 48 hours prior to the meeting beginning.

The most important thing that affects how a meeting works, is the way the chairperson handles it. In most churches it will be the minister that is in the chair, and there is no doubt that this is where your "ministrycraft" really shows. No one can teach you how to chair a meeting. But it is something that you can practise and get better at, though there is no doubt that there are some people who seem to have a natural aptitude for it. That is not confined to the church and experience in the "real" world has shown that in business and in public authorities like the NHS chairing a meeting well is every bit as much of a hit and miss affair as it is in the church. Whether it is the House of Commons, the Health Board, the District Council or the local branch of the Cat Protection League a good chairperson is worth his or her weight in gold! I make no claim to being in that category but I do know a good chair when I meet one, and on that basis would offer you some pointers to success in this important area:

1 Learn from other people. Don't just moan when you get home that "the chairperson was rubbish tonight" but ask yourself why, and whether there is anything you can learn from that. Even

more important, when you strike gold in the person of a "natural", don't just sit back and enjoy it, but try to analyse what it is that he or she does which makes them so effective.

2   Practice may not make perfect but it can make you a lot better. If you are given the opportunity during your training or probationery period (and you should be) to chair meetings, take them. Ask your supervising minister for feedback afterwards and just as important ask someone in the meeting (preferably not another minister) to observe how you handle it and comment to you afterwards. If you are in a charge it is still not too late to get help though it requires an element of humility to suggest you might not be perfect! There must surely be someone that you can trust enough to give you some pointers without it completely destroying your ego.

3   Make good use of the Agenda. There is no point having an Agenda if you do not stick to it but there is always someone who will want to jump around it or ignore it altogether. "That matter will come up under item 7 on the agenda and we shall deal with it then" keeps the meeting in good order. As well as that the sequence in which items come up on an Agenda usually has some logic to it and it makes sense to stick to it. For example, there is no point in discussing repairs to the church tower before the Treasurer has given his report on the up-to-date financial situation.

4   Make it clear that you are in charge. It is fine for the minister to be pally with everyone, but at a meeting there is a need for the chairperson to make it clear, in the nicest possible way of course, that he or she is in control. Despite what some people seem to think, that is best done not by being pompous or overbearing but simply by being firm, courteous and fair. Trying to be too nice is every bit as bad as being horrid and objectionable - the real knack or *craft* is in finding the middle way between these two extremes.

That means above all being absolutely straight with everyone and being consistent both throughout the meeting and from meeting to meeting. It can come as a real shock if the chairperson who is always bending over backwards to accommodate everyone suddenly says, "I am ruling that out of order!" to one of the stalwarts of the Kirk Session. He may be perfectly right but it may not seem so if he or she has not been consistently firm on previous occasions.

5   Achieve a balance. If you look at the Agenda for a meeting it does seem to consist largely of items to be reported or items to be decided. In theory there is not any need for there to be any talking at all - just hear the reports and make the decisions. But we all know that that is not the way meetings are, and that it is the discussion of items after they are reported or before they are decided which is the real "meat" of the meeting (or maybe it should be "meet" of the meeting!) Suppose the Kirk Session has before it a proposal to change the time of the Morning Service on a Sunday from 11 am to 10.30 am. There will be an item on the Agenda to this effect. It is possible that if the suggestion has come from a Committee or Team that a paper outlining the reasons for the proposal will have been circulated beforehand. Either way there is likely to be a fairly full discussion of such an important matter with views being expressed both for and against the change. This is an important part of the decision-making process because listening to what other people say helps everyone to make up their minds. Not everyone comes to the meeting with a definite view and even those who do may change it in the light of new information or ideas. For example the information that the local bus service which brings a proportion of the worshippers to church, does not have a service which fits the proposed 10.30 am start and that all those coming by bus would be in the church by 9.50 am may turn a number of session members against the proposal who had previously been in favour. All sorts of views

will be expressed on such an issue and all sorts of information will be presented, not all of it necessarily relevant or helpful! The crucial role of the chairperson is not only to keep firm but courteous control of this discussion but to judge when it is time to move on to making the decision. That is the skill - knowing when to draw the discussion to an end so that those attending feel the topic has had a good airing, but before the more voluble start to repeat themselves.

6   Don't be afraid of a vote. It is a mistake to think that the discussion should go on and on until a consensus is reached. Human nature being what it is that may never happen, and there is nothing wrong with taking a vote, so long as it is understood that once the decision is taken it is binding on every one. If the Kirk Session votes by 30 to 15 that the time of the morning service should be changed from 11 am to 10.30 am then that becomes the official policy of the Kirk Session which every member should support. If you discover that members of the Session are undermining the decision after it has been reached then it is time for a quiet word with them behind the bike shed!

7   Make your views known. Procedurally of course this is entirely wrong! Correct procedure on meetings suggests that the Chairperson should be completely unbiased and not express his or her view on the topic being discussed, focusing entirely on controlling the discussion and the subsequent decision making. But in the church context that is nonsense, because it is usually the minister who is in the chair, and it is often the minister who knows more about the topic being discussed than anyone else at the meeting, or at least as much! If the minister follows correct procedure and does not impart his or her thoughts on the matter, the meeting is deprived of what is probably its most helpful source of advice. If for example the minister does not tell the Kirk Session what he or she thinks about changing the time of the

Service from 11 am to 10.30 am and what kind of reactions he or she may have received to the proposal from members of the congregation, the Session is denied an important viewpoint. The secret of course, is the way in which the minister who is also Chairperson actually does this! If he or she speaks eloquently and at length in support of a proposal the Kirk Session is considering or actually raises it on the Agenda, it then becomes very difficult for other people to disagree because they seem to be not only disagreeing with the proposal but going against the minister. If it eventually goes to a vote, then that begins to feel not just like a vote on the issue but a vote of confidence (or no confidence!) on the minister himself or herself. Of course there may be occasional times when an issue is of sufficient importance that the minister is ready to put himself or herself in that exposed position, but usually it is better avoided. However it is still possible to feed into the discussion, some of your own thoughts and feelings so long as it is done in a fairly low-key way so that it has the feel of "another person at the meeting expressing their thoughts on the matter" rather than "the minister pronouncing the final word on the matter." There is nothing wrong with saying when a suitable opportunity occurs, "I have some thoughts on this matter which might be helpful at this point." A wise Session Clerk may provide the opportunity for you by saying, "It would be good to know what the minister thinks about this." The aim is to affirm the right of the Kirk Session to reach decisions as a body, while ensuring at the same time that the views of everyone who wants to express them have been heard, including the minister.

Chapter 18

O & M - Sub Committees, Teams and Working Groups

More and more churches, especially those with very large Kirk Sessions are opting to do a lot of their work in sub-committees. Personally I like the term "Team" because it gives a feeling of togetherness and of movement. "Sub-Committee" somehow suggests that it will go on and on for ever and nothing will ever happen! Presbytery and General Assembly provide good models here but also make the pitfalls clear. The obvious advantage of Teams is that all the detailed thinking and discussion can go on in a small group, who can then bring their finalised proposals to the main body for approval. This is a much more fruitful way of dealing with an issue, because a small Team can really get into the nitty gritty of it and come up with solutions for possible difficulties whereas if the raw proposal goes to the main body direct it will lead to a lengthy debate, focus often on some minor matter, and may result in the proposal being rejected over a detail that could have been sorted out. The other thing is that most church leaders feel that they are making a much fuller contribution to the work of the church if they are in a small Team working together. It also means, and this can be important in a big congregation, that office bearers actually speak to each other and get to know each other!

If you decide to take the route of having "Teams" it is not difficult to identify the main ones. In Appendix K I have outlined a list of possible Teams for the Kirk Session (unitary) largely drawing on the pattern at King's Park, Glasgow to whom much thanks. Before you dive for cover at the length of the list bear in mind that a substantial number of these teams should only have two or at the most three members, and few of them should require the continued presence of the minister. Naturally every congregation will be different and want to have some distinctive Teams but there are some general points worth considering if you are using this kind of structure or thinking of introducing it.

1 It makes it very important that there are regular meetings of the parent body (Kirk Session) so that the Teams can report. It is helpful if this is done even if the particular Team is in the middle of considering some big issue - it lets everyone know where they have got to and everyone can begin to think about it. It may even be that the Team will want to sound out the parent body on some aspect of their ongoing work.

2 However if Teams are beginning to work successfully it is worth considering whether these regular meetings of the Kirk Session might be held once every two months rather than monthly. This makes it possible to use the free night or nights to have Team meetings and keeps the time commitment under control. In many congregations this is becoming a very big problem as able people are increasingly under pressure in their jobs. Of course if all the Teams are going to meet at the same time, some of them would require to meet in private homes, and that can be very successful.

3 It may be that at a particular stage a Team will wish to meet with another Team. For example, if a Team has been set up specially to look at the Church Magazine, it will be useful for them to meet at an early stage with the Team which considers all aspects of publicity and communication in the church.

4 Once a "Team Culture" is established in a congregation, it makes it easy to set up small Ad Hoc Teams to deal with particular issues. The Fabric Team is fine to deal with all aspects of maintaining the Church Fabric, but if it is discovered that the church tower is in immediate danger of falling down, a small Team set up to deal only with this urgent matter, may be more effective in getting action quickly.

5 The members of Teams will normally be drawn from the parent body and include appropriate officials. Thus the Finance Team will include the Treasurer, WFO Convener and Stewardship Convener. But there is no reason why it cannot also include other members of the congregation who are not Session members. This is a good way of introducing new people and new ideas and of using all the talent that is available - something we are still not very good at despite all our "stewardship of time and talents" campaigns. A good way of setting up Teams initially may be to have a mini "stewardship of time and talents campaign" amongst your church leaders. This may help to identify who has time to spare for important tasks that are likely to be time consuming, who will be most effective in which team, and who might be good as Team Leaders.

6 If the Team system is to work well, it requires an overall attitude of trust. Teams should have the authority from the parent body to deal with minor matters without having to constantly come, cap in hand, for authorisation. On the other hand, major proposals obviously need to come to the Kirk Session for approval, but even then there needs to be an attitude of trust that the Team has done its work, has thought through the issues, and that their proposals can be relied on. That does not mean it should always be a rubber stamping job, but there should be good reason for going against a proposal presented by a Team. It is a matter of getting the

balance right and being willing to trust each other - not a bad idea for a church!

7 As far as pitfalls are concerned I suppose the main one is that if a Team is particularly active and comes up with a lot of ideas, those who are not on that particular Team may feel a bit excluded. That is why it is important that there is effective reporting back from the Team to the main body, so that everyone can "own" the decision which is being made. The other obvious pitfall is that instead of being very active, a Team may be totally inactive, either because the Team Leader does nothing, or the other members of the Team do not respond. In either case the problem needs to be raised at the next meeting of the parent body, but if hurt feelings are to be avoided it needs to be done in a sensitive way, with some preparation behind the scenes beforehand.

8 One of the disadvantages of our management structure in the Church of Scotland in the past has been that everything in the church's life was supposed to be either a matter for the Kirk Session or the Congregational Board. Fortunately this false division into "spiritual" and "temporal" can now be avoided through the new Unitary Constitution which means that one body, the Kirk Session, is responsible for all aspects of the church's life and work. This also encourages an element of flexibility to make the best possible use of the human resources that are available.

Chapter 19

O & M - Church Office and Church Secretary

One of the most effective ways of handling the O & M in the church is to have a church office and a church secretary. Like so many ideas this one has probably come from the USA where even rural churches have an office and secretary as a matter of course and large city charges have a plethora of administrative staff housed in plush suites of offices. Before we assume that because it comes from the USA it must inevitably be a bad idea, it is worth considering this as a possibility. Having myself been sold on the idea on an exchange visit to the USA in 1992, and having then gone through the process of setting up a church office and employing a secretary here, I have to say that this was the single most important change for the better during my seventeen year stint in my last charge. It has huge advantages both for the church and for the minister and it is worth looking at some of them, while recognising that there can also be disadvantages.

Church Office and Secretary - For

1 It means that the Church has an open door and a public face during the week. Most Church of Scotland buildings are sealed up from Sunday to Sunday and look totally dead and unwelcoming. The presence of a Secretary in an office, with an

appropriate sign outside of course, means that the church is seen
to be alive and functioning.

2   A church office provides a focus for members of the congregation
as well as the public at large. People often feel that they do not
wish to disturb the minister with a minor matter. A quick phone
call or visit to the church office means it can be resolved.

3   The Church Office and the Church Secretary can fulfil an
important pastoral role just by being there. If you live alone and
never see anyone except when you go out for your shopping, it
can make all the difference to drop into the church office for a
brief word with the Secretary who knows you by name. As long
as you don't keep her or him back from keying in the Kirk
Session Minutes!

4   The Church Secretary can carry out a large number of
administrative tasks more quickly and efficiently than if they are
being done on a voluntary basis by individuals. These can
include - printing and distribution of minutes of Kirk Session and
Teams, maintaining the Congregational Roll, preparing the
weekly Worship Leaflet with Announcements, and completing
returns to Presbytery and General Assembly.

5   The Church Secretary can build up a working knowledge of all
aspects of the congregation's life so that she or he is able to
answer questions and resolve problems without the minister being
involved. As a result the load is spread and the church is seen to
be not entirely centred on the minister.

6   A reasonable filing system, either paper or computerised, means
that the church has accurate records of what it has been doing and
this can be invaluable in planning ahead. Think for example how
helpful it would be in planning your Elders' Conference this year
if you could look back in a file at the content of all the Elders'
Conferences that have been held over the last ten years, with File

Notes giving comments on how successful they were and what problems turned up in organising them. Or think how useful it would be in considering your theme for this year's Holy Week Services if you could look back at what had happened in Holy Week for several years back, particularly if you have only recently become the minister.

7 A Church Secretary can be worth her or his weight in gold in a supporting and supportive role to the minister. Although members of your congregation can be willing and helpful it is sometimes more trouble than it is worth to phone someone up, explain what you want done, and coordinate with them. As a result most ministers, most of the time do it themselves, or land it on their wives or husbands when they come home from work. With the support of a Church Secretary all sorts of minor tasks can be carried out easily and quickly, saving the time and energy of the minister for other more important things. You want a large box at the church door on Sunday covered in christmas paper to receive gifts for children in a local children's home. Instead of having to get hold of someone to do it and having to be there to let them into the church with it once its done, or spending time doing it yourself instead of making that important visit, a quick word with the church secretary who may even know where the box is from last year, but if not has christmas paper on hand and cellotape at the ready, and can make a brief visit to Tesco or Asda to find a suitable box, and the job is done. Multiply that one simple task by a thousand and you begin to discover just how valuable a church secretary can be!

Church Office and Secretary - Against

1 Clearly the most important negative is cost. There is a fairly substantial initial capital cost involved in setting up an office and equipping it properly, and once you have someone in post there is

the ongoing cost of salary and national insurance as well. Some congregations will not be in a position to undertake this kind of expenditure on top of all their "normal" commitments. But before you decide yours is in that position it is worth working out exactly what is involved. A Church Secretary employed for two mornings a week, say for three hours each morning, and at a rate of £7.00 per hour (national minimum wage currently £5.73 per hour 2009) will cost the Church something like £2184 per annum plus additions. It is not a huge amount and even at that level of hours she or he will make a huge contribution to the life of the congregation and in making best use of the minister's time which will be out of all proportion to the cost.

2   Another potential hazard can arise if you choose the wrong kind of person as the Church Secretary! It is a job which requires tact, confidentiality, a sense of humour and infinite patience, and these qualities do not grow on trees. On the other hand because it is likely to be a part-time position and probably in the mornings it is likely to suit someone with experience who is looking for a way back to work after bringing up children, assuming for the moment that the person concerned is female. Just for the record there is absolutely no reason why the Church Secretary should not be male. You may find that although the hours are small, that very fact along with the "interest" factor of an unusual position results in a surprising number of applicants. But the choosing has to be done carefully and thoroughly even though it seems to be "just a wee job at the church." That means going through the whole procedure of drawing up a proper Job Description and having it approved by the Kirk Session; drafting an Application Form so that you get all the right information from applicants; then advertising, short-listing and interviewing before making an appointment. You can find details of a Job Description for a Church Secretary at www.churchofscotland.org.uk – Support and Services Council – Central Services Committee. It is always

worth checking the claims applicants make as to their word processing skills with a short test and taking up references, before finally making up your mind. It goes without saying that while the minister should be involved in all of this as he or she will be the person who works most closely with the Church Secretary, it should not be left to the minister alone. This is an ideal situation to set up a special Team who will take the project through all its stages. It is particularly important that the interviews are conducted by at least two people and probably three, one of whom should be the minister, and the other two active church leaders, like the Session Clerk or the Treasurer. In this way the decision is shared, and the appointment is seen to be church based. In other words it is not the "Minister's Secretary" that is being appointed but the "Church Secretary."

3 A third potential difficulty can be that everyone (or one particular person) wants to tell the Church Secretary what to do! This can happen particularly in middle class congregations with members who have been used in their work to having people working under them or in congregations with a large number of retired members - and that is probably most! If this kind of thing happens, the Church Secretary is uncertain where his or her responsibility lies and the result is confusion or even bad feeling. A good Church Secretary can even be lost because of this - "I seemed to be always trying to please everyone and there was never enough time" is the kind of feeling that leads to a resignation. This can be avoided if it is made clear in the Job Description to whom the Church Secretary is responsible and exactly who is in charge of the Church Secretary. It may not necessarily be the same person in relation to different aspects of the work, but that needs to be spelt out. The Job Description also needs to make clear the procedure for dealing with any problems or disputes so that on the one hand the Church Secretary does not feel impotent if someone in the congregation is making their life

hell, or on the other hand the minister does not feel impotent if the Church Secretary is making his or her life hell. We shall look more closely at some of the issues relating to all church employees in chapter 21 - "The Church as Employer".

Volunteer Church Secretary

Some Churches recognise the need for a Church Office and a Church Secretary, feel that they cannot meet the cost of a paid appointment, and decide to opt for a volunteer or volunteers. I have no direct personal experience of this though at second hand my impression is that it can vary hugely in effectiveness from extremely successful to total disaster. There are a number of very obvious pitfalls which need to be taken into account if you are thinking of having a volunteer as Church Secretary.

1 Inevitably it means a loss of status in the role of Church Secretary. Paying someone to do the job is a way of saying that it really matters. Conversely doing the job with volunteers reduces its importance, no matter how much you may protest to the contrary.

2 You cannot expect someone to be there on set hours and set days every week if they are not being paid. No matter how committed the person is at the beginning inevitably things will crop up and just when you need the help desperately it will not be there.

3 If as often happens no one is willing to commit to six or nine hours a week on a voluntary basis you may finish up with two or even three volunteers. It then becomes very difficult to maintain consistency in the way things are done, even small but important things like the way in which the church telephone is answered. It also means that a lot of time can be spent just handing over from one volunteer to another, or keeping some kind of log book or record.

4 It is almost bound to reduce the potential help that the Church Secretary gives to the Church and in particular to the minister. "I can't ask her to do that, she's a volunteer" is likely to be a reaction in at least some situations.

Having said all that about pitfalls I know there are situations where a volunteer Church Secretary works very successfully and makes an enormous contribution to the life of the church. It just depends!

Working with the Church Secretary

We hinted at the possibility of a bossy member of the congregation making unacceptable demands on the Church Secretary and the importance of defining clearly the lines of responsibility in relation to the post. But the most important aspect is how the Minister and the Church Secretary work together. Clearly there is little point in even thinking about appointing a Church Secretary if the Minister is totally against the idea or cannot understand why it is being suggested. There are ministers who work best on their own, like to be in control of everything, and do not want someone else knowing where they are going and what they are doing. On the other hand many ministers today will have come from a working environment where they will have had secretarial or other kinds of assistance and will take to it like a duck to water. However there are certain fairly unique features about the Minister and Church Secretary relationship which need to be thought about if such an appointment is going to work well.

Give It Time

A good Church Secretary working effectively will save the Minister a great deal of time, but it is necessary to give some time to it in order to reap the reward. This is particularly true in the early stages, when working practices and procedures are being established. The

Minister and the Church Secretary need to get to know each other
and become friends - this is much too close a relationship to be
maintained on a purely professional basis.

Be Willing to Offload

There is a kind of "martyrdom" aspect to ministry which seems to
make ministers feel they ought to try to do everything or nearly
everything themselves. Of course you can get a certain amount of
sympathy from your congregation if you are seen to be constantly
running yourself off your feet, but it is doubtful if that is good for
you or the congregation in the long run. For most ministers, it is
quite hard to hand things over to someone else and that is the
particular skill we need to learn if we are going to make the best use
of a Church Secretary. In fact it is not just a matter of handing things
over, it is then being able to trust that they will be dealt with
satisfactorily without checking up on them. That comes only with
time and as the relationship develops that absolutely essential
element of trust. When you think about it, although there are some
things a minister does which are quite unique and nobody else can
do, there are also lots of things we get involved in that any sane,
normal person with a modicum of intelligence and commitment can
do for us, if only we are prepared to let them.

Give of Yourself

There is no doubt that you will gain most from a Church Secretary if
you are prepared to give something of yourself to it. For example, if
you know you are going to be in Edinburgh all day at a meeting of
the Ministries Council tell your Church Secretary. Then if an urgent
situation arises, for example arrangements for a funeral, the
Secretary knows where you are, and will have a good idea when you
will be home and where you can be contacted. "You should be able

to get him by dinner time and I suggest you ring the manse" is so much more helpful than "I don't know where he is or when he will be back. Maybe you will be able to get him tomorrow." In fact a good Church Secretary who is experienced in these matters can go ahead and make the funeral arrangements so long as you have agreed some ground rules beforehand. But that can only happen if you do the next thing regularly.

Check Diaries

If there is one single thing that is important in working with a Church Secretary it is to have a regular diary check. This is best done weekly as otherwise the information is not up-to-date, and first thing on a Monday morning is as good a time as any unless that is the Minister's day off. Of course this assumes that the Minister keeps a Diary, either paper or electronic, which details all of his or her appointments and commitments and that the Church Secretary also keeps a Diary which ideally includes all that is going on in the Church. It is a comparatively easy exercise once a week, to go over the diary appointments to ensure that both the Minister and the Church Secretary know what is happening. Of course you do need to go over more than one week ahead, but it is not necessary every week to go right to the end of the year! Once this is done, the Church Secretary is in a position to do a great deal for the Minister, in responding to enquiries about availability and in arranging meetings and appointments. The other advantage of a weekly diary check is that it identifies tasks which have to be undertaken. Once you have noted that the monthly meeting of the Kirk Session is on Wednesday evening, the Church Secretary can contact the Session Clerk and draft the Agenda, let the Minister have sight of it and print off copies.

Trust and Confidentiality

The importance of trust in the relationship between Minister and Church Secretary cannot be over-emphasised. The Minister needs to know that when he shares information with the Church Secretary which may be confidential or pastorally sensitive it is not going to be repeated to the next person who comes into the Church Office. This is so important that it needs to be talked about explicitly by the Minister and Church Secretary at a very early stage in the working relationship. It cannot be left to chance nor can you assume that it is understood. It is not just a simple matter of "never tell anyone anything" because if the Church Secretary follows that rule his or her usefulness will decrease by leaps and bounds. It requires careful thought and discussion to draw up a Confidentiality Code that is useful and workable. If the Minister comes into the Church Office and tells the Church Secretary that his son has been in trouble with the police, he needs to know that it will go no further. On the other hand a phone call from a District Elder seeking an update on the illness of a member when the Elder has previously discussed the situation with the minister, can be an opportunity to pass on helpful information.

Once the congregation realise that the Church Office is not going to be a source of juicy gossip about life in the manse or unlimited information about the goings on in the community and the illnesses and ailments of all and sundry, they will come to appreciate that the Church Secretary can be entrusted with confidential information in the absence of the Minister. Sensitive messages can be taken and passed on, information and advice can be given, and in this way the Church's care and concern can be shown through the Church Office. This pastoral role which the Church Secretary can fulfil needs to be taken account of. An apparently unimportant phone call or an apparently aimless visit may be an individual's way of asking for help and a good Church Secretary will always have the time and the sensitivity to respond appropriately.

The Church Office

If you have decided to put forward a proposal to your congregation to appoint a Church Secretary you will also have to think about a Church Office. That can be a major stumbling block if your church premises are particularly cramped and every square metre is already being used. On the other hand if there is a real will to make this happen, it is often surprising how the space can be found. One of the lessons learned recently on moving on retirement from a commodious manse into a new bungalow, has been to evaluate the importance of reserving precious and expensive space for purposes which only occur rarely. For example it is fine to have a posh dining room for the odd occasions when you want to impress visitors, but when space is at a premium is it not better to have a study/office type of room which will be useful to you every day and let the visitors eat in the kitchen? The same question arises over the guest bedroom which is only used once or twice a year - do you want to keep that space you have paid for nearly always empty? Would you not rather have a workshop/dress-making/computer room that will be of real use? If we begin to ask the same kind of questions about the church premises, we will quickly discover that there are spaces that are reserved for particular functions which for most of the week lie empty. Working on this basis, some churches have converted the Minister's Vestry in such a way that it can be used as a Church Office through the week but still fulfil its role in providing the Minister with a private place before worship. Others have recognised that a particular space which is used on a Sunday morning for a children's group can be reduced in size without reducing its effectiveness, and the detached part can be converted into an office. However, no matter how big the manse is, think carefully before deciding to situate the Church Office there. It does mean that one of the big advantages of a Church Office which is that the church premises are opened up, is lost. It also means that a lot of activity focuses on the manse - that may be fine by you if you are single and rattling about in the place, but it may not be so good when your successor arrives with a husband, four children, and two Labradors! Anyway it is good for every minister if the Manse can at times be more of a place to get away *from* work rather than a focus *for* work.

Assuming you have found a suitable space, the next step is to convert it into an office. This means first of all, that it has to be reasonably bright and comfortable, with good lighting, heating and floor covering. If the church does not have a phone connection this will need to be put in at this stage. Then, the space needs to be furnished and equipped. If money is tight it is worth investigating some of the office suppliers who provide second-hand furniture and equipment. The essentials include a good-sized desk with a proper office chair, at least one filing cabinet, a storage cupboard, and a computer complete with printer. Don't forget that unless the lighting is exceptionally good a desk lamp is a must, and that if people are going to call into the office to speak to the Secretary, at least one additional chair and preferably two is needed. Do not be too quick to accept offers of discarded furniture or equipment from members - they may not be suitable, can give the new office a second-hand feel from the beginning, and are difficult to get rid of once they are accepted. It always surprises me that some people see the church as a dumping ground for all their rubbish! If they do not want the particular items in their own home or office why are they OK for the Church? If it really is God's house, nothing but the best should be good enough, and maybe that applies to the office as well as the sanctuary! It is not difficult to set up the Office but it does cost money - there is no way of avoiding that if you are going to do it properly.

Setting up an office in these days of IT means that you can go as far down that road as you want to. It is perfectly feasible to have a completely paperless office where all the records are computer generated and this reduces greatly the need for storage such as filing cabinets. On the other hand you may decide to take a middle road and set up a paper filing system for some aspects of the church's work. It may be for example that your Fabric Team will want to keep the actual copies of quotes from companies if they are undertaking a major repair or building project. The most important thing to recognise right from the outset is that every ten years or so it will need a good clean out by someone ruthless, otherwise the church office will gradually disappear amidst rows of filing cabinets.

The question of what particular brand and size of computer to purchase is one that will probably cause considerable interest in the Congregational Board. The relationship between the human species and the computer is a unique one, and one tiny aspect of that is that individuals are very anxious for reasons of prestige to be seen to be knowledgeable about them. So if you suggest HP, someone will want to buy Dell, and if you suggest AMD someone will want to buy Epson. You need to be aware of what is happening - it is much more important than it appears on the surface, and unless you have very definite ideas yourself it may be worth giving in! What is much more important than brand names is to ensure that the computer has sufficient capacity (hard drive) to more than meet your conceivable needs for at least five years, that the memory (RAM) is big enough to allow the processor itself to work quickly and efficiently, and that the graphics are of sufficient quality and with an adequate memory to cope with any illustrations you might want to use in the church magazine and other publicity material. There is no doubt that the best way of going online is now Broadband and this means that the church phone is not tied up whenever the computer is online. The use of Emails is a quick, cheap and accurate way of communicating with the huge advantage over a phone call that you can check later exactly what was said. Just as the Church of Scotland is now communicating with all the Presbyteries in this way, the future is undoubtedly going to be that Presbytery will communicate with its congregations in this way, and that churches will communicate with their members in this way. Being online means of course that the church can have its own website and we have discussed some of the possibilities of that in chapter 14. Even fairly standard computer packages are perfectly capable of coping with this.

The choice of printer can be particularly important in the Church Office, simply because the originals may well be used to run off numerous copies of the worship leaflet or the church magazine. A good sharp original will produce better quality copies even if the equipment is less than state of the art. Of course if you are using state of the art equipment the document as prepared on screen will be transferred directly to the duplicator or copier without producing a paper copy at all. But it is worth thinking carefully about the purchase of the printer before opting for the cheapest available. An "All-In-One" Printer, Scanner, Fax and Copier can be a particularly good buy for a church office as it combines all these functions in one piece of equipment, costing less and taking up less space. The one drawback with some of these is that the ink cartridges can be fairly pricey.

Chapter 20

O & M - Making It All Work

Having covered most aspects of O & M it is worth stopping for a moment to look at the big picture. The key to running a church successfully is of course team work, and one of the ways to make a team effective is to keep everyone informed. From that point of view you may find that the weekly meeting between the Minister and the Church Secretary to check diaries can be made more useful by pulling in other people to be present. For example if your Session Clerk is fully involved and plays an important role in the congregation, it will be extremely helpful to have him or her at the weekly meeting. If you have a person other than the Church Secretary whose job it is to organise all the bookings for the use of the church accommodation both for church groups and community organisations, a lot of questions can be resolved immediately if he or she is present. In one congregation in the USA of which I had experience the Church Sexton (as they called him - we would call him the Beadle or Church Officer) was present for part of the meeting so that he knew what layout of tables and chairs was required for various occasions taking place during the ensuing week. It may all sound a bit over the top - "The Monday Morning Management Team Meeting!" - but the reality is that an hour spent in this way can save everyone a lot of time for the rest of the week, and just as important foster that "feel good" factor which is so important to the smooth running of the church organisation.

Going back to what we said earlier about the importance of sharing information on the pastoral side and the need for a regular weekly meeting of the pastoral team (always bearing in mind the need for confidentiality) it may be that the "management" meeting and the "pastoral" meeting can be organized together for a Monday morning. In about two hours much of the church's life for the following week can be considered and organized. That cannot be time wasted when we realize that from then on, a team of people are working productively because they understand clearly what they are doing and how it fits into the big picture.

Chapter 21

O & M - The
Church as Employer

As we develop new styles of ministry and see the role and operation of the church in new ways, we get more involved in the whole business of the church employing people on a paid basis. Most congregations have traditionally had a paid Organist and Beadle as well as Minister, but now it is possible that a Church Secretary, Youth Worker, Community Worker or Associate Minister may also be employed either by one congregation or on a shared basis with other congregations in the area. Sample contracts for Church Officer, Church Cleaner, Church Organist or Choirmaster, Church Secretary and Youth Worker, are all detailed on the Church of Scotland website under the Central Services Committee of the Support and Services Council. But a good contract is only the beginning of an individual church recognising its responsibilites as an employer and taking them seriously. One of the weaknesses of government by committee is that no one person sees it as their job to look after the Beadle or the Organist and when a problem arises the only way of dealing with it is to raise it at a full meeting of the Kirk Session which is hardly ideal. If for example the Organist feels quite justifiably that he or she is not being paid a fair rate for the job it is very difficult to raise such an issue at a large meeting or to have it raised on your behalf. If the minister feels that the Beadle is not really pulling his or her weight there has to be a better way of handling it than to open it to general discussion at a meeting.

Just as important as specific issues or problems that can arise is the way it feels to be an employee of the church. It can be only too easy for those whom we employ to undertake specific tasks to feel that no one really has responsibility for them or is interested in them, and that the only time the Church seriously thinks about them is the annual review of their salaries when the impression is so often given that it is a matter of "how little of an increase can we get away with?"

There are two important issues here. First there is no point in us preaching a Gospel of justice, fairness and compassion if we do not follow these principles ourselves in the way we treat our employees. Second we have to recognise that as soon as we become employers even of part-time personnel, we have to adhere to all the rules and regulations that apply and all the employment legislation that has been enacted. Of course it is not the job of the minister to undertake all of this himself or herself but it may be necessary for the minister to ensure that this whole area of the church's life is taken seriously and handled properly. In the rest of this chapter I would like to suggest three ways in which this can be done in practice.

1 The Personnel Team

In many congregations you may be fortunate enough to have one or more people who are experienced and knowledgeable in the whole area of employment and who may be willing to put their skills at the service of the church. Such a person can form the nucleus round which you can set up a small team, probably three people at the most, who will be the first point of contact with those whom the church employs. It would then be the job of the Personnel Team to deal with any problems or difficulties which arise and if necessary to make recommendations for change. The most important quality required of the members of the Personnel Team is the ability to keep their own counsel so that church employees can feel comfortable about approaching them. If we go back to the case of our underpaid organist, assuming that the congregation has a personnel team in place, it would be much easier for the individual to discuss the problem in confidence with the three members of the team, who could then make a recommendation to the full Kirk Session. But if a Personnel Team is working effectively then it should be possible to avoid situations of conflict altogether by having a proper written Job Description drawn up when the person is first employed, and by having a regular annual review for each employee of the church.

2 Job Description

When we were discussing the role that a Church Secretary might fulfil in chapter 19 we touched on the need for a proper Job Description. As well as all the important legal requirements that you will find detailed in the sample Job Descriptions on the church website there needs to be a general statement about the nature of the particular job, who the employee will be working with, and the qualities you consider the job requires. If the Church is looking for someone as Secretary who can take initiative and will respect confidentiality then that needs to be said. Beyond that the more detail you can give of the duties you want the person to carry out the better, so that anyone interested in the job can get a "feel" of what is involved and so that any uncertainties can be resolved quickly. If the new Beadle says "I didn't know I had to ring the bell and I've got a sore back" then "Ringing the Bell" should have been in his or her Job Description!

However it is also important to leave room for growth and change. After a period of time the Church may decide to set up its own web-site and that one of the duties of the Church Secretary will be to update it weekly. From that point of view it is good if the Job Description can include some kind of open-ended statement like "Other duties as required."

3 Annual Review

The main purpose of having a Personnel Team in the Church is not to deal with problems when they arise, but to avoid having problems arise! The best way of doing that on an ongoing basis is to take the time at least once a year to sit down with the employee and talk to them. Whether you call this process Annual Review or Assessment or Appraisal is not important - what does matter is that it is done regularly and done well. Here are some pointers which may be of help.

a) The Annual Review should NOT simply consist of putting the employee through the third degree about how they are doing their job! Obviously if there are areas where it is felt performance could be improved these should be raised, but only in the context of a much wider look at all aspects of the post and the person, raising such questions as -
   "Are you enjoying your work with us?"
   "How are you getting on with the the other members of the team?"
   "Are there any problems you are having about the job?"
   "Are there ways in which you think we could do things better?"

By raising such questions the Annual Review becomes an opportunity for everyone to have a fresh look at one particular part of the Church's work and perhaps to discover areas for improvement. It also helps to create the feeling that everyone is working together rather than it being a case of "them and us".

b) The Annual Review of those employed by the Church should be carried out by the Personnel Team alone and not with the Minister present. After all the Minister could be the biggest problem the Organist has about her job and she is hardly likely to speak about it if the Minister is present! It may be necessary for the Personnel Team to quietly take some soundings from those directly working with the employee, always bearing in mind that too much emphasis should not be placed on such second-hand information, and that any serious complaints need to be properly checked out. If members of the congregation are constantly complaining that the Beadle is rude to people it should not be too difficult to establish the truth of such an accusation!

c) Two members of the Personnel Team should carry out the Annual Review with the individual concerned - any more than that could be intimidating - and maximum effort should be made to create the right atmosphere so that it can be a relaxed and informal occasion. The Church Vestry with no heating on a cold winter's night is far from ideal!

d) Undoubtedly the most important thing about the Annual Review is that it should be totally confidential. It is only if the person concerned is sure that what they say will go no further than the room they are in that they are likely to share the things that are troubling them or even make suggestions for improvements. This means that one of the main jobs of the members of the Personnel Team is to check out whether the individual wishes them to take any particular matter further. Sometimes all that is needed is to get something off your chest and to know that someone else is aware of the problem. On other occasions it may be that having given the issue an airing the person will want the Personnel Team to take it further. Whether anything is going to be done and what is going to be done needs to be made absolutely clear. "We agree that you are being underpaid as the organist and we propose to raise this at the next meeting of the Kirk Session with a recommendation for a 10% increase. Is that OK with you?" That leaves no doubt about what is being proposed.

Chapter 22

The Ministry of Time

It sounds a bit over the top to talk about a "Ministry of Time" unless of course it is a new government department dedicated to getting politicians to talk less! But when I think about my years in ministry there is no doubt that the single biggest challenge I faced was in time management - never having enough time to do all the things I wanted to do, never having enough time to do things as well as I wanted to do them, and constantly having to make difficult decisions about priorities simply because there was not enough time. If you have stayed with me up to this chapter you are probably thinking "He's got a nerve talking about the ministry of time after all the things he has suggested we ought to be doing." Of course that is absolutely true and that is exactly why time management or if you like the ministry of time is so important - the more enthusiastic we are about the craft of ministry the more important it is that we manage our time well. Most of us when faced with time pressures simply resort to working more hours and that is OK up to a point, and that point comes when we find ourselves working 24/7, never having a break of any kind, and never spending any time with our family or friends. When we get to that stage we all know we are heading for trouble and we need to step back and take a long hard look at our time management. This is a huge topic and deserves a book to itself but I would like to share a few ideas which have helped me to manage my time better. But first let us be honest and admit that the nature of ministry is such that it cannot all be tidy and pre-planned no matter how well organised we are. There are bound to be times when chaos reigns and if we are being true to our calling and responsive to people's needs then that is as it should be. On the other hand it is sad to see a minister who seems to be constantly chasing his or her tail, who rushes from one crisis to another, and who claims never to have time to do any of the things he or she wants to do. So with that proviso here goes!

A Weekly Framework

Ministry is exciting and challenging simply because you never know when you get up in the morning what is going to happen. On the other hand ministry can be stressful and worrying if every morning when you get up you have no idea what you want to happen. In other words, it is good to have some kind of framework for your week, always allowing for the possibility of something coming up that changes everything. Once settled into your first charge it is good for every minister to sit down with a blank sheet of paper, line out a seven day week, dividing each day into three blocks of morning, afternoon and evening, and then write in the things that are essential and unavoidable. It may surprise you how few there are - apart from conducting worship on a Sunday the only other regular commitment you may have to fulfil is a weekly Vestry Hour. After that it is a matter of deciding when it suits best to do the things that have to be done but with some flexibility as to time, such as preparing for worship, pastoral visiting and so on. We talked in chapter 1 of the importance of setting aside a regular time each week for preparation for worship and this should be one of the first things that you put into your framework - whether you mark off the whole of Monday, Thursday or Friday for it or not is a matter of personal choice. You will soon realise that you are not just deciding when things should be done within your weekly framework but also what your priorities are as well. For example if you block off every Tuesday morning to visit local schools then that becomes one aspect of ministry to which you are committing yourself at a significant level. But before all the blocks on all the days of the week are filled there is something else you must do at an early stage - decide on your time off. Ministers are probably getting better about taking time off than they used to be, but many still find it difficult - the calvinist work ethic combined with a sense of guilt about actually enjoying ourselves are no doubt at least partly responsible. Anyway everyone knows that adequate time off is essential not only for your own health and welfare but for your family and friends and also in the long run for the congregation you are serving. A minister who is anxious, stressed and even burnt out because of over-work is of little good to himself or herself, or to his or her congregation. There are two things to be decided about time off – how much and when. Most working people have two days off each week and I do not see any reason for ministers to be any different from that. Actually deciding when to take time off depends on your circumstances - Saturday is often a good day if you have a working partner and school age family, Monday or Friday can be candidates if you are single, your partner does not work, or your children are under school age. When you take time off does not matter - the main thing is to do it and to tell your congregation that you are doing it. A congregation will soon learn that Saturday is not a good day to phone the manse because it is one of "the minister's days off." Of course this assumes that Sunday is a full working day, and that is not always the case, so bear in mind that if you lead worship in the morning and then have the rest of the day relaxing with your family that really means you have had a half day off.

Once the essentials are included in your weekly framework you can look at other priorities you may have in your ministry and decide what can be undertaken. It is also important to have some flexibility built into the week so that the unexpected can be coped with without it meaning that you immediately eat into your precious free time. And here we have to be honest with ourselves - there is no way that everything we want to do can be fitted in - so the guiding rule in all of this has to be - Prioritise! Prioritise! You can see one possible suggestion for a weekly framework at Appendix L just to get you thinking.

Forward Planning

"Easter is in two weeks and I haven't done a thing about it!" That is a recipe for stress and too often that is where we find ourselves. We get Christmas over though it always takes a week or two to recover, we keep saying to ourselves - "I really must think about Easter", there is a busy time with funerals as often happens in January and February, we are off for a few days at a conference or in-service training and suddenly it's Easter! That seemed to happen to me every year not just in relation to Easter but Advent, Christmas, and Lent as well until I made up my mind to do something about it. That "something" was to blank off in my diary two periods in the year (late summer for Advent and Christmas, and January/February for Lent and Easter) which would be devoted entirely to advance preparation of worship or other activities such as Lent Bible Studies. In each case the periods were of two or three days and in each case I went away to one of the many conference or retreat centres that are available. If you work along with others in a team to prepare worship then obviously it is essential that they are included. But even if that is not the case there is tremendous value in doing this with someone else who shares your thinking and approach. The best ideas often come from sparking off each other in the quiet of the evening sitting at a log fire, sipping a glass of wine! Before we start to feel guilty and accuse ourselves of self-indulgence ask anyone in business or industry and they will tell you that this is exactly what they do - take the Management Team to a hotel for two or three nights and talk about how to improve their product or sell more of their product. Tell the congregation why you are going away and what you are doing and it will make them realise just how seriously you take your job of leading them in worship. If you are in the habit of planning worship and preaching in blocks - a series of six sermons on St Paul, or seven sermons on the miracles of Jesus for example, the same procedure can be followed. It goes without saying that if the minister and other members of the team are going to be absent from the parish arrangements need to be made to provide adequate cover. Perhaps a reciprocal arrangement with a neighbouring minister will allow you both to do some forward planning and get rid of that nagging anxiety!

Getting Away From It All

As well as times when it is worth going away to do some forward planning, there should also be times when we go away simply in order to get away from everything. Of course holidays with our partner, family or friends, can be invaluable in recharging the batteries but there is also a place for something more focused such as a Spiritual Retreat to a residential centre which specialises in this area. There are now a number of such places with varying programmes to suit different tastes. I personally have found The Bield at Blackruthven a source of strength and support in my many visits there both for forward planning and retreat. It offers daily prayers both morning and evening, opportunity for a range of artistic activites, swimming and walking, one-to-one support when requested, and a warm and caring atmosphere in attractive surroundings. It is worth taking time to find somewhere that suits you so that when the need arises the decision to go is made more simple. For some all that is really needed is somewhere to sleep with meals provided so that the time is our own to use as we see fit. For others a more structured programme of study and devotions will be more helpful. The main thing is to see this as an opportunity for spiritual strengthening and growth - this is not the time to be working on your Christmas programme or restructuring your congregation's administration!

Hobbies and Interests

Naturally we all agree that we should have hobbies and interests that we pursue, just as we all agree that "all work and no play" is a bad idea. But the reality is that it is extremely difficult in ministry to find the kind of time that is needed to pursue a hobby seriously. So do we simply give up trying? My view is that even if we can only manage a little time, it is important to pursue some interest outside the church and its life. The reason is obvious - focusing on church and nothing but church means we lose perspective and eventually become rather boring people. There are some hobbies that lend themselves more readily to ministry. If you enjoy fishing for example you can do that at any time you find you have a few spare hours - it does not require planning ahead or finding other people to do it with. The other good thing about a hobby is that it gives you something very definite to do on your time off. There is always a temptation to say - "I'm too busy for time off this week" - but if you have already planned a hill-walking outing or a round of golf with some friends it is that much more difficult to put it off.

Doing Nothing!

Well, why not? What about sitting in the garden for an hour? Or talking to your wife? Or playing a game with your grandchildren? Or walking down to the paper shop to buy a paper? There have to be times when we are human enough to actually do nothing without feeling great mountains of guilt! And these may be the times that are important, when we realise we are part of a family or a community. So while all the planning is important it is also important that our "ministry of time" gives us permission now and then to do nothing and enjoy it.

Study Leave

Ministers in the Church of Scotland are fortunate in having a recognised and approved arrangement for Study Leave, which not only provides the necessary time but also some finance to go with it. For some years I acted as the Study Leave Coordinator for our Presbytery and it was a source of continuing astonishment to me that so few ministers made use of their right to Study Leave. Nothing stands still in ministry any more than in any other profession because the world in which we minister is constantly changing. Study Leave is a recognition that we need to be constantly improving, developing and honing our "ministrycraft" skills.

I suspect that one difficulty about Study Leave is deciding what to do with it. The Ministries Council has made it easier for us by laying on a variety of courses and conferences which meet the criteria for Study Leave. But what about taking the bull by the horns? The words "Study Leave" suggest *time to study* so why not do just that? There must be some topic you have met in your ministry which has made you think - "I wish I had more time to go into that more fully" or "that is a really interesting idea if only I could pursue it." The opportunity is there at least for ministers in the Church of Scotland. Other denominations may have similar Study Leave schemes, and if not I would be surprised if most congregations would not respond positively to a request from their minister for an annual allocation of Study Leave. One year my Study Leave provided me with the opportunity to write a paper on "Communion - Belief and Practice" which explored the relationship between what we believe about Communion and what we actually do when we celebrate

Communion, and included an Order for Home Communion which I subsequently used regularly. I have included this as Appendix M not because I have ambitions to be a theologian but in the hope that the Home Communion Service may be of use. Another year I made use of my Study Leave to explore the whole question of the relationship between Pastoral Care and Worship which led in turn to me writing the Service of Prayer and Blessing referred to in chapter 12 which I also used regularly and is detailed in Appendix F. The message about Study Leave is very simple - USE IT! The message about the "Ministry of Time" is simple too - You cannot do everything so prioritise, prioritise!

Chapter 23

The Stress Factor

One of the themes that ministers often return to in their sermons is the humanity of Jesus - how he was a real person who had ups and downs like the rest of us - losing his temper, feeling lonely, needing to chill out. What we sometimes forget is that ministers are real people too and that we too have our ups and downs just as Jesus did and just as everyone else does. We catch colds, we break limbs, we get depressed, and we feel tired. Like many other people with demanding jobs we can also feel the effects of stress. Jesus seems to have had his own way of dealing with the pressures of being a popular preacher in great demand by going off on his own whenever the opportunity arose. But how do we deal with stress in ministry and what choices are available to us?

The first and obvious thing is to recognise where we are and what is happening. That can be quite hard sometimes - how can we be tired or burnt out when we are doing God's work? The reality is that whatever we are working at - minister, doctor, teacher, taxi driver, checkout assistant - all of us can feel the effects of stress if we work too many hours, try to do too much, and worry about what is not getting done. In many ways men and women in ministry are more open to stress than most for two reasons - there is no one to tell us what to do and when to stop, and there are always more things to do than we can possibly achieve. Given these two factors a certain level of stress is almost inevitable in ministry and maybe it helps to keep us on our toes! It becomes a problem when the stress gets too high, and begins to affect how well we are functioning. That is the time when we have to make the difficult judgement that our stress level has gone too high for comfort and do something about it. For many of us one good barometer of our state of stress is how well we are sleeping. As long as we get a good night's sleep it is amazing what we can cope with through the day. Once our sleep pattern is seriously upset on a regular basis, probably because we are worrying about all the things we have to do, then it is time to take action.

The right way to deal with stress is to give in to it! The wrong way to deal with stress is to keep struggling on in the hope that it will go away - it won't. In fact it will get worse and we will find ourselves in a downward spiral of things that are pressure points for us and the worry that goes with them. There are a number of different ways of giving in to stress or rather recognising and responding to stress in our lives that has become destructive rather than creative, and the way we choose will depend on all sorts of personal factors and circumstances.

Running Away from Stress

Sometimes the best thing to do if we are under extreme stress is just to run away! Of course that is a bad way of putting it because it suggests we are being defeated by it, while in fact it may be exactly the opposite - that the best way to score a victory over stress is to get out from under it. It may be a few days away on your own to a favourite haunt, it may be a visit to family or friends in another part of the country, it may be a week in a hotel with your nearest and dearest, sometimes the simplest solution is the best and when things are piling on top of us and threatening to drag us down, some time away will make a huge difference not just in having that much-needed rest but also a chance to stand aside from the spinning top and begin to see what was happening to us. So running away can be a very positive way of dealing with stress.

Getting Help with Stress

Of course there are times when running away is not enough. The pressures have become so great, the level of anxiety has become so high, the whirling top is spinning so fast, that when we go away we simply take it all with us and spend these precious days of escape by worrying even more. That may be the time when it is necessary to seek help from someone who has the necessary skills and training to help you look at what is happening, examine the causes, and work out a strategy for dealing with your stress. There are many different counselling agencies and individuals available but the best starting off point is undoubtedly the "Ministries Counselling Service" organised by the Ministries Council of the Church of Scotland. You can self-refer to the Service but access is usually through referral by the appropriate staff of the Council, by Presbyterial Advisers or through the Occupational Health Scheme. Ministers in the Church of Scotland are fortunate in that members of staff in the Ministries Council provide caring and support in crisis situations which is second to none. But it may not even require the input of a professional counsellor - it may be that the Presbytery Adviser or a friend or colleague can provide the sympathetic and patient listening which is all we really need to sort out the issues for ourselves. What is certainly true and along with many others I can personally testify to it, is that having someone to talk to whom you trust and respect can totally change everything. That is why it is important to recognise that there are times when we need help with stress without in any way feeling that so doing is a sign of weakness or an admission of defeat.

Avoiding Stress

If we agree that ministry is probably a fairly stressful occupation, then as well as identifying ways of dealing with the stress when it arises, it makes to sense to look at ways of trying to stop it happening altogether or lessening its effect. Cliche but true - "Prevention is better than Cure." I have no doubt that there are all sorts of different approaches but I shall limit myself to outlining two with which I am familiar - The Support Team and The Triad.

The Support Team

Just as it can be good to talk things over with a counsellor or friend, it can also be helpful to share your problems, anxieties and difficulties with a small group of specially chosen people. The important thing about a Support Team is that it is not something you try to set up when you are facing crisis, it is up and running before you need it. A good Support Team will be quite small, (probably three people is enough) will be totally confidential, and will be very carefully chosen. It is important to distinguish between this kind of Support Team which is offering pastoral care to the minister, and the kind of Support Team which is concerned along with the minister in looking at a particular part of the Church's life. A Worship Support Team for example has a valuable contribution to make but this is not what we are talking about here. Whether the Support Team for the minister is best drawn from members of the congregation or from outside the congregation is open to debate, but the crucial thing is to choose people who are up to the job - trustworthy, wise, preferably knowledgeable about the Church, and with no axes to grind. By meeting regularly and talking openly and honestly about what is going on in the church and what difficulties there are for the minister, an atmosphere of mutual trust and confidence can be established, so that when trouble looms, the minister can turn to this group in the confidence that their role is to give him or her their care and support. If a Support Team works successfully it can be a great asset to the minister and therefore to the church. It has to be said that the biggest problem with any such group is to ensure confidentiality. It is extremely destructive if the minister bares his soul to his Support Group only to discover that what he has said becomes the subject of gossip at the street corner.

The Triad

It is because confidentiality is so crucial that The Triad has developed as another way of providing support for ministers in the hope that acute stress can be avoided. The basic principle is the same - that sharing with others in an open and honest way can resolve many of our worries and anxieties before they become critical. As the name Triad suggests this support group is made up of three people, all of them ministers, and each one of them offering support to the others. An ideal arrangement is for three ministers from different towns or areas to form a Triad so that each one has a fairly objective perspective on the circumstances of the other two, rather than all three being drawn from the same town or the same Presbytery. Once again, a regular meeting, probably monthly, enables the group to grow together in trust and respect. Once again, confidentiality is crucial and it must be clearly understood from the beginning that nothing that is talked about in the Triad will be spoken about or even mentioned outside the group. My own experience of a Triad of which I was a member for over fifteen years along with Duncan McClements and Leith Fisher, both sadly no longer with us, was that it was good at all sorts of levels - a couple of hours away from the parish with two friends, an opportunity to talk about church issues in an open and honest way, and when it was really needed support and understanding and wise counsel from two people whom you really trusted. That was when the Triad came into its own - when someone in your congregation was making life impossible for you and you could not discuss it with anyone else; when you were worried sick about how you had handled a pastoral situation; when the conflicting pressures of work and family were really getting on top of you; when your faith seemed to be crumbling a bit at the edges. Thankfully we found that there were some months when the Triad would meet and no one was in crisis! That provided an opportunity to chat about a book we had read or some issue that was making the headlines in Presbytery or General Assembly, or even to share advice about filling in our Income Tax Returns.

At the risk of repeating myself and boring you to bits, I am certain that the tired old cliche "Prevention is Better than Cure" is entirely true about Stress. So set up your Support Group or Triad now!

Chapter 24

"Ministrycraft" - Go For It!

So there it is - my view of at least some aspects of the "craft" of ministry. We have ranged far and wide but before we end let me emphasise two things which I said in the Introduction. One is that this is an essentially personal view - it is not an academic exercise in any sense and I am quite ready to be told that I have contradicted or ignored others who are much wiser and more knowledgeable. I have not set out to make a contribution to any ongoing academic debate but to set up my stall largely on the basis of practical experience. The other is that I do not claim in any sense to have covered every aspect of ministry but have focused on some of the things that seem to me to be important - I leave it to you to decide if I am right or not.

Ministry is not easy but it is exciting. Difficult at times, downright frustrating often, lonely occasionally, and always just a bit beyond your grasp. Being a minister is a constant process of learning, training and gaining in experience, and that is what makes it a very special "craft" and a very rewarding one. Enjoy the times when things are going well and do not be afraid to have fun in your ministry - remember that there is room in every "craft" for a few incantations and a spell or two! If the difficulties are great, the rewards are enormous - the unique privilege of leading people in worship, the humbling yet elating realisation that your pastoral care has made a difference, and above all doing what you know God wants you to do. Enjoy your "Ministrycraft"!

Appendix A (page 8)

Nigel Robb has kindly given me access to a very full list of books about worship and books containing prayer and worship resources – thank you! You will find this list on my website at www.johncnicol.com.

Appendix B (page 34)

A Meditation for Good Friday focusing on some of the simple items surrounding the Crucifixion

Introduction
Congregation   There is a green hill
Prayer

The Wine
The Wine is brought to the cross
Voices
Reading   Luke 23 : 13 – 26
Silence with music
Choir   O sacred head sore wounded

The Hammer and the Nails
The hammer and the nails are brought to the cross
Voices
Reading   Luke 23 : 27 – 38
Silence with music
Choir   O Lord of life and glory

The Robe
The Robe is brought to the cross
Voices
Silence with music
Congregation   O sacred head sore wounded

The Crown of Thorns
The crown of thorns is brought to the cross
Voices
Silence with music
Choir   What language shall I borrow

The Spear
The spear is brought to the cross
Voices
Silence with music
Choir   Be near me Lord, when dying

Prayer
Congregation   When I survey the wondrous cross
Blessing
Choir   O sacred head sore wounded

(You will find the full script for this service on my website under "Ministrycraft" – www.johncnicol.com)

Appendix C (page 34)

"I to the Hills Will Lift Mine Eyes" – A Meditation for Good Friday

<u>Outline of Service</u>

Music for Good Friday
Welcome
Congregation   I to the hills

<u>The First Hill – Sacrifice</u>
Narrative and Readings   including Matthew 27 : 32f
Prayer
Congregation   There is a green hill

<u>The Second Hill – Challenge</u>
Narrative and Readings   including Mark 3 : 13f
Prayer
Congregation   Will you come and follow me

<u>The Third Hill – Devotion</u>
Narrative and Readings   including Matthew 5 : 1f
Prayer
Congregation   From heaven you came

<u>The Fourth Hill – Mission</u>
Narrative and Readings   including Matthew 28 : 16f
Prayer
Congregation   Rise up, O men of God

The Hill of Good Friday

Narrative and Readings	including Matthew 27 : 33 and 39
Prayer	
Congregation	My song is love unknown

Blessing
Music for Good Friday

(You will find the full script for this service on my website under "Ministrycraft" – www.johncnicol.com)

Appendix D (page 34)

"Laughing at God" - A Meditation for Good Friday

Music for Good Friday
Introduction
Congregation   There is a green hill
    Laughing at Others   Embarrassment
    Solo   Help us accept each other
    Laughing at Others   Disbelief
    Solo   Help us accept each other
    Laughing at others   Change
    Prayer
Congregation   Help us accept each other
    Laughing at Jesus   Observers   (Matthew 9 : 18f)
    Organ   Lifted high on your cross
    Laughing at Jesus   Neighbours   (Mark 6 : 1f)
    Organ   Lifted high on your cross
    Laughing at Jesus   Pharisees   (Matthew 12 : 22f)
Congregation   Lifted high on your cross
    Laughing on Good Friday   The Soldiers
    Solo   O sacred head sore wounded
    Laughing on Good Friday   The Passers-By
Congregation   O sacred head sore wounded
    Laughing at God   Ourselves
    Prayer
Congregation   We sing the praise of him who died
Blessing

(You will find the full script for this service on my website under "Ministrycraft" – www.johncnicol.com)

151

Appendix E (page 35)

Outlines of Advent Themes

1 Preparing for Jesus

A model nativity scene is set up in the church, but without the manger, straw or baby.

Advent 1	A bed for the baby	The manger is added – simplicity of his birth
Advent 2	Straw for the bed	The straw is added – reality and ordinariness of his birth
Advent 3	Clothes for the baby	The swaddling cloths are added – his common humanity
Advent 4	The baby arrives	The baby is added – the preparing is complete

2 "I am the light of the world"

Each Sunday an Advent Lantern is carried down the aisle to the front of the church.

Advent 1	The Light of Life
Advent 2	The Light of Trust
Advent 3	The Light of Strength
Advent 4	The Light of Love

3 The Christmas Pudding

A giant Christmas Pudding is made from wood, card and papier mache. It is in four quarters with an opening on the inner surface of each quarter to contain an object.

Advent 1   A Candle – I am the light of the world
Advent 2   Statue of a Shepherd – I am the good shepherd
Advent 3   Bread – I am the bread of life
Advent 3   Road Sign – I am the way

4 The Decorations on the Christmas Tree

Each Sunday in Advent a decoration is added to the Christmas Tree in the Church.

Advent 1   An angel – Came to Mary
Advent 2   Tinsel – symbol of kindness
Advent 3   Star – followed by the wise men
Advent 4   Lights – Jesus, the light of the world

5 Following A Star

Each Sunday in Advent a man or woman brings a star to the front of the church and tells his or her story of "following my star."

Advent 1   Ninian
Advent 2   Elizabeth Fry
Advent 3   Elsie Inglis
Advent 4   Ray Davey

(You will find the full script for these Advent themes on my website under "Ministrycraft" – www.johncnicol.com)

Appendix F (page 61)

SERVICE OF PRAYER AND BLESSING

Welcome 1 (to be used when only regular attenders are present

Welcome to our Service of Prayer and Blessing this evening. You will find the order of service in the worship leaflet and we hope that you will join us for a cup of tea afterwards.

Welcome 2 (to be used when new attenders and/or visitors are present)

I would like to welcome you to this Service of Prayer and Blessing this evening. You will find the order of the service in the worship leaflet and I would like to mention one or two things before we begin.

This is a service of worship to God like all church services. But it is a service of worship in which we hope to open ourselves especially to the love and peace and healing of God and to share his blessing. That means there will be some traditional bits like any other service as well as some bits which are new and different.

In particular I would like to mention the prayers for others in which we shall not only pray in general terms for those who are ill and those who are facing problems, but we shall pray more specifically for individuals by name. We do this because the person concerned or someone on their behalf has asked for our prayers.

The other thing in the service I would like to mention is The Blessing. After a few words of introduction anyone who feels that they would like to share in a blessing is invited to come forward.

Two other things about the Service. We will remain seated for some of the songs and this will be announced. There will be a cup of tea afterwards and we hope you will join us.

LET US WORSHIP GOD!

Praise

Prayer of Approach and Confession

"The Lord is near. Do not be anxious about anything, but in everything, by prayer and petition, with thanksgiving, present your requests to God. And the peace of God, which transcends all understanding, will guard your hearts and your minds in Christ Jesus."
(Philippians 4 : 5 - 7 NIV)

Let us pray.

Our loving Father, we your children, gather together to worship you, knowing that you are near to us. Help us now, knowing your nearness, not to be anxious about anything, but in confidence to bring to you our prayers, to bring to you our problems, to bring to you our anxieties, to bring to you our hopes, and to bring to you our dreams. May we know your peace in our minds, in our hearts, and in our bodies, the peace which comes to us through Jesus Christ.

Let us open ourselves to that peace, asking that God will remove all the obstacles we have placed in the way.

Father, remove all that we have placed in the way of the peace you offer to us through your Son Jesus Christ:

- our selfish and self-centred living
- the hurts and wrongs we have inflicted on others
- relationships which are bruised and broken
- our own failures and weaknesses which we have not been able to admit and accept.

Lamb of God, you take away the sin of the world.

Take away our sins tonight, take away all the obstacles we have placed in the way, and grant us your peace, through Jesus Christ our Lord, Amen.

Praise

Bible Reading followed by Talk or Meditation

Praise

Prayers

We are all going to share in the Prayers for others and for ourselves. After each individual or group of people is named I shall say "Father, in Jesus name" and you should respond "Bring healing, bring peace."

We shall then share in the prayers of thanksgiving. To the words "In Jesus name" please respond with the words "We give you thanks."

> "The Lord is near. Do not be anxious about anything, but in everything by prayer..... present your requests to God." (Philippians 4 : 6 NIV)

Let us pray.

Lord God, we know that you are near. We bring to you now, knowing your nearness, those who are in need of your presence, in need of your power, in need of your love, in need of your healing, in need of your wholeness, in need of your peace.

We pray for ....and for ....

| *Leader* | : | Father in Jesus name |
| *Leader and People* | : | Bring healing, bring peace |

We pray for .... and for ....

| *Leader* | : | Father in Jesus name |
| *Leader and People* | : | Bring healing, bring peace |

We pray for ....and for.....................

Leader	:	Father in Jesus name
Leader and People	:	Bring healing, bring peace

As we pray for them we pray for all who are ill, distressed, in pain, anxious, unhappy, lonely.

Leader	:	Father in Jesus name
Leader and People	:	Bring healing, bring peace

We pray for doctors and nurses and for all those who seek to cure and to relieve the suffering of those who are ill.

Leader	:	Father in Jesus name
Leader and People	:	Bring healing, bring peace

We pray for all the pastoral and healing care that is expressed through our church, and for our minister, our pastoral assistant, our elders, and our church visitors.

Leader	:	Father in Jesus name
Leader and People	:	Bring healing, bring peace

We pray for those who care for loved ones at home and for all the individuals and agencies who offer support.

Leader	:	Father in Jesus name
Leader and People	:	Bring healing, bring peace

We pray our own prayers in this time of silence.......

Leader	:	Father in Jesus name
Leader and People	:	Bring healing, bring peace

Leader	:	Father, for your love for us gentle as a shower healing our pain binding our wounds in Jesus' name
All	:	We give you thanks.
Leader	:	Father, for your love for us sure as the dawn

		transforming our darkness revealing your truth in Jesus' name
All	:	We give you thanks.
Leader	:	Father, for your love for us mercifully steadfast calling us to you raising us up in Jesus' name
All	:	We give you thanks.

We say together the prayer that He taught us.

Our Father, who art in heaven,
hallowed be thy name.
Thy kingdom come.
Thy will be done on earth
as it is in heaven.
Give us this day our daily bread.
And forgive us our debts,
as we forgive our debtors.
And lead us not into temptation,
but deliver us from evil.
For thine is the kingdom,
and the power,
and the glory,
for ever. Amen.

Praise

The Blessing

There will now be a time of silence with some quiet music. During this time of prayer and meditation if you would like to share in a moment of blessing I invite you to come forward. You can do this either standing or kneeling, by hands placed on your head or your shoulders, with your hands held, or without any contact. Please say which you would prefer when you come forward.

If you do not want to come forward, please do not feel that you are under any pressure to do so. You may like to use this quiet time to reach out to God with your own prayers and to know the peace that he brings through Jesus. You can minister to those who do come forward by praying for them. At the close of the Service everyone in church tonight will share a blessing in the words of the Benediction.

This is an opportunity to bring to God yourself - your pain, your hope, your bewilderment, your trust, your uncertainty, your confidence, your sorrow, your joy, your anger, your faith, your needs, your enthusiasm, and to know the blessing that God offers to each one of us through Jesus.

(The organ plays softly as blessings are shared)

Spirit of the living God,
present with us now,
enter you, ...*(first name)*
body, mind and spirit
and heal you of all that harms you,
in Jesus' name,
Amen.

(Once all so wishing have shared in the Blessing there is a time of silence while the organist plays softly the music of "Abba Father, let me be, yours and yours alone" - played twice)

Lord, you are near us now. May your presence go with us as we return to our homes, to our work, to our living together and may we know the light of Jesus illuminating our way. Enfold us in your arms so that we may share in the joy of knowing that we are your children, and that we can be full of faith and hope and trust in Jesus Christ our risen Saviour, Amen.

Praise

Benediction

Go and know that the Lord goes with you. Let him lead you each day into the quiet place of your heart where He will speak with you. Know that he loves you and watches over you, that he is with you always wherever you may be and however you may feel. And the blessing of God, Father, Son and Holy Spirit be with you all now and forever.

Amen.

(You will also find the full script for this service on my website under "Ministrycraft" – www.johncnicol.com and you are welcome to download, print and use it.)

Appendix G (page 61)

Readings, Prayers and Blessings

for use at times when death is near

Readings

The Lord is my shepherd; I have everything I need..........	Psalm 23	(GNB)
The Lord is my light and my salvation; I will fear no one.......	Psalm 27: 1, 4,5	(GNB)
"For one brief moment I left you; with deep love I will take you back......	Isaiah 54: 7 – 10	(GNB)
After the Sabbath, as Sunday morning was dawning...	Matthew 28: 1 – 10	(GNB)
Who, then, can separate us from the love of Christ?......	Romans 8: 35 – 39	(GNB)
May you always be joyful in your union with the Lord....	Philippians 4: 4 – 7	(GNB)
I heard a loud voice speaking from the throne....	Revelation 21: 3 – 7	(GNB)

Prayers

With family and friends when death is approaching

Our loving God, we need your help and your support. We are uncertain what to think, unsure about what to pray for. We find it difficult to cope with the suffering of *John* (and even more difficult to accept that soon *he* will leave us). Yet we are confident that even in the midst of his pain and our distress you can bring your light, your love, and your peace, and we ask you to do that for us now. Still our anxious hearts with that peace which only you can give, the peace that comes through Jesus Christ.

Be with *John* at this moment and in the hours/days that lie ahead, that he too may know the peace and comfort of your presence, and go forward in trust and confidence to be with you. In Jesus name we pray, Amen.

With the individual family and friends when death is approaching

Our loving Father, we come to you now, in our need and our pain and our uncertainty. We feel confused and helpless, not sure what to think or what to believe. But we are sure of your love for us, made real in Jesus, and so we know that we can hand over to you all our confusion and helplessness, all our doubt and all our fear. Father, help us to do that now, so that the darkness of this time may be illuminated by the peace that only you can bring.

Be with your child *John* and help *him* to know that he is supported and upheld by the love and care of *his* family/friends. May he feel the strength and comfort of your everlasting arms, and find in you his peace, through Jesus Christ our Lord, Amen.

With family and friends when death is close

Our loving God, we come into your presence now, bewildered, hurting and uncertain. We do not know what to do or what to say. But we believe that you are with us now, that even at this moment you reach out to us with your loving arms, offering us the comfort and the strength of your presence. Help us to hand over *JOHN* into your care, knowing that you receive *him* and that with you *he* is safe. Accept *him* into the light of your presence which is beyond all pain and all suffering. We ask it in the name of Jesus, Amen.

With the individual family and friends when death is close

Loving Father, we come close to you, bringing you our suffering and our anxiety, asking that you will be with us and especially with your child *John*. Reach out to *him* with the strength and the gentleness and the completeness of your love so that *he* may know beyond any doubt that you are waiting to receive him. Grant *him* at this time courage to go forward, patience to wait on your purposes for *him*, and the peace that comes from drawing close to you. In Jesus name we pray, Amen.

With family and friends when death is past

Our loving Father, we draw near to you in this time of sadness, bringing you our pain and our despair at the loss of *John*. We find his death difficult to accept, but we trust and believe that *he* is even now in your presence, and that all *his* pain and suffering are over. We thank you for all that *his* life has meant to each one of us and for all the good memories that we can share together in the midst of our sadness. Be with those who loved *John* most at this time and help us all to find the faith and the strength to cope with the difficult days that lie ahead, through Jesus Christ our Lord, Amen.

Blessings

May your hearts and minds know
the peace of God
which leads away from anxiety,
and the wisdom of God
which lights the way ahead. (Rowland Croucher)

May the Lord bless you and guard you;
may the Lord make his face shine on you
and be gracious to you;
may the Lord look kindly on you
and give you peace.   (Common Order)

To the mercy and protection of God
we commit you.
The blessing of God almighty,
the Father, the Son and the Holy Spirit
rest upon you and remain with you always.   (Common Order)

Several of the Blessings contained in "The Pattern of Our Days –
Liturgies and Resources for Worship" edited by Kathie Galloway
and published by The Iona Community are particularly suitable for
this purpose – especially nos 72, 73, 74, 76, and 77.

Appendix H (page 66)

FUNERAL

NAME   :
ADDRESS   :

AGE   :
DATE OF BIRTH   :
DATE OF DEATH   :
PLACE OF DEATH   :
CHURCH CONNECTION   :

NEXT OF KIN   :
RELATIONSHIP   :
ADDRESS   :
CONTACT TEL NO   :

UNDERTAKER   :
TEL NO   :
DAY & DATE OF FUNERAL   :
PLACE(S) OF FUNERAL   :
TIME(S)   :

    ☐   CHURCH
    ☐   PARLOUR
    ☐   CREMATION
    ☐   BURIAL
    ☐   INTERMENT OF ASHES

HYMNS AT CHURCH   :

HYMNS AT PARLOUR   :

HYMNS AT CREMATORIUM   :

FAMILY DETAILS

NOTES

Appendix I (page 70)

Funeral Reading

Nothing can fill the gap when we are away from those we love, and it would be wrong to try and find anything. We must simply hold out and win through. That sounds very hard at first, but at the same time it is a great consolation, since leaving the gap unfilled preserves the bond between us. It is nonsense to say that God fills the gap; he does not fill it, but keeps it empty so that our communion with another may be kept alive, even at the cost of pain. The dearer and richer our memories, the more difficult the separation. But gratitude converts the pangs of memory into a tranquil joy. The beauties of the past are not endured as a thorn in the flesh, but as a gift precious for its own sake.

(Deitrich Bonhoeffer)

Appendix J (page 99)

KIRK SESSION AGENDA

Monday 2 March 2009 at 7 pm

1 Opening Devotions
2 Welcome and Apologies
3 Approval of Agenda
4 Approval of Minutes of Meeting held on ....
5 Matters arising from Minutes
6 Correspondence
7 Report from Presbytery Elder
8 Report from Treasurer
9 Kirk Session Teams – report as required (see Appendix K)
10 Interim Report from special Working Group on "Future Vision"
11 Worship for Holy Week and Easter Sunday
12 Date of next meeting Monday 6th April 2009 at 7 pm
13 Closing Prayer

Appendix K (page 106)

Possible Sub Committees/Working Groups/Teams of Kirk Session (Unitary Constitution)

1	Christian Education
2	Finance
3	Forward Planning (including themes for Kirk Session Conferences, setting priorities, future vision)
4	Gardening
5	Gift Aid
6	Health and Safety
7	Mission
8	One World
9	Pastoral Care
10	Property
11	Safeguarding
12	Security
13	Housekeeping
14	Social and Fund Raising
15	Staffing
16	Youth
17	Worship

Appendix L (page 133)

WEEKLY FRAMEWORK

	Morning	Afternoon	Evening
Monday	Team meetings	Flexi - time	OFF
Tuesday	O & M	Pastoral visiting	Meetings night
Wednesday	School(s)	Pastoral visiting	Vestry Hour Bible Study Group
Thursday	Worship preparation	Worship preparation	Worship preparation (if necessary)
Friday	Preparation for School and Bible Study Group	Flexi - time	OFF
Saturday	OFF	OFF	OFF
Sunday	Worship etc	Worship etc	Worship etc

Appendix M (page 137)

Home Communion Service

Extract from Study Leave Report : "Communion – Belief and Practice" September 1998

While the need for our theology of communion to match our practice remains the same whether it is celebrated in church or in a private home, the circumstances are so different that they seem to me to require special consideration in shaping a "Liturgy for Home Communion". I would suggest the following as possible guidelines in structuring a communion service for home communion:

1 The basic elements of Communion - Take, Bless, Break and Share should be included.

2 The liturgy should include some expression of a link between the home communion and the congregation's communion to give the person receiving home communion a sense of being part not just of the universal church but of his/her own local church.

3 The language should be simple but dignified so as to fit the domestic situation but at the same time give due worth to the sacrament. Overly "churchy" language would be inappropriate as would forced informality.

4 Home Communion is often very intimate and moving and the prayers in particular need to give due recognition to the distinctive feel of the circumstances.

5 It would usually be appropriate (but not always) to include prayers for the person receiving communion and possibly for

his/her family, neighbours, etc, bearing in mind that the person is likely to be either elderly or ill.

6 It has to be realised that the person receiving communion may be nervous or uncertain and it is important that the liturgy as far as possible puts the person at his or her ease and contains no surprises. For that reason responses should not be introduced in home communion unless there is a long tradition of these being used in the worship of the congregation. The use in the liturgy of familiar words, for example the 23rd Psalm and the Lord's Prayer can be very supportive.

In preparing my Order for Home Communion I have tried to take these guidelines into consideration. I have also referred to the following:

1 Book of Common Order 1994 Church of Scotland Fifth Order for the Lord's Supper for Use at Home or in Hospital

2 Three Orders for Holy Communion 1986 - Panel on Worship, Church of Scotland Order for the Celebration of Communion with the Housebound or Sick

3 Scottish Liturgy - Scottish Episcopal Church Communion of the Sick

4 Uniting in Worship 1988 Uniting Church in Australia Communion beyond the Gathered Congregation

5 Worship Now 1972 - St Andrew Press A Home Communion

I have noted too that this is not something new but that some form or order for the visitation of the sick or communion with the sick occurs in much earlier liturgies both of the Church of Scotland and the Church of England. For example the liturgies drawn up in the reign of James VI entitled

"The Booke of Common Prayer and Administration of the Sacraments with Other Rites and Ceremonies of the Church of Scotland as it was Sette Down at First, Before the Change Thereof Made by ye Archb. of Canterburie, and Sent back to Scotland" included *"The Order for the Visitation of the Sicke."*

Likewise the Book of Common Prayer of 1662 contained both *"The Order for the Visitation of the Sick"* and *"The Order for the Communion of the Sick"*, the latter with the following delightful footnote:

"In the time of the Plague, Sweat, or such like other contagious times of sickness or diseases, when none of the Parish or neighbours can be gotten to communicate with the sick in their houses, for fear of the infection, upon special request of the diseased, the Minister may only communicate with him."

Order for Home Communion

Welcome

Jesus said : "Where two or three come together in my name, I am there with them." (Matthew 18 : 20) (GNB)

In the joyful presence of our risen Lord, we gather at his table to share in the sacrament of Holy Communion, knowing that as we do this we are united with our fellow Christians who gathered at his table *this morning/yesterday/last Sunday* in ……….. *Church* and with all those who love and serve Jesus Christ around the world.

Prayer

Let us pray:

Our loving God, we praise you for all the ways in which you make known your love for us - in the wonder and beauty of the world around us; in the love and friendship which we share with each other, in the possibilities for goodness that you kindle within each one of us. We thank you that your love is made known to us in a special and wonderful way in Jesus your Son who is our shepherd and our king. We admit to you now that we do not live up to all the love you have for us, that we misuse the resources of our world, that we are often selfish and petty in the way we behave even to those who love us, that we are too ready to smother the flame that is your goodness within us. Father, forgive us. Forgive us for all that we have done and all that we have been that is out of tune with your purpose for us. As we gather at this table, renew us in faith and in love, through Jesus Christ our Saviour, in his name we pray, Amen.

Readings

Let us listen to God's word.

. . . .

. . . .

Thanks be to God for his word to us.

Invitation

Jesus invites us to this table to share the bread and wine which make his presence real to us and bind us together in his love.

The grace of the Lord Jesus Christ be with you.

Communion Prayer

Let us pray:

Lord our God, we thank you for Jesus Christ, your Son and our Saviour. We thank you that he lived on earth like us, that he knew disappointment and pain as well as joy and hope, that he blessed the children and healed those who were ill, that he reached out to those who were outcasts from society. We thank you that he was so ready to obey you that he died on a cross for us and for all the people of the world. We thank you that he rose from death and is alive today, blessing and healing and reaching out to the whole world, and that he is with us now at this table, reaching out to us, loving and forgiving us.

We join with the people of the Church through the centuries and all round the world to say together these ancient words

Holy, holy, holy Lord,
God of power and might,
heaven and earth are full of your glory.
Hosanna in the highest.

Blessed is he who comes
in the name of the Lord.
Hosanna in the highest.

Heavenly Father we pray that your Holy Spirit will bless us and bless this bread and wine as we share together in communion so that we may know in our minds and hearts the reassurance and comfort and strength of your Son Jesus Christ our Lord, who gave himself for us, body and blood, and so that we may look forward to being with him in the glory of your kingdom. We pray together as he taught us:

Our Father, who art in heaven,
Hallowed be thy name.
Thy kingdom come.
Thy will be done in earth, as it is in heaven.
Give us this day our daily bread.
And forgive us our debts, as we forgive our debtors.
And lead us not into temptation, but deliver us from evil;
for thine is the kingdom and the power and the glory,
for ever, Amen.

Breaking of Bread

We do this because Jesus wants us to. On that last night together with his disciples he took a piece of bread, said the grace, broke it, (breaks bread) and shared it with them with these words : "This is my body, which is broken for you. Do this in memory of me." In the same way, after the supper, he took the cup (raises cup) and said, "This cup is the new covenant in my blood; do this, whenever you drink it, in memory of me."

Lamb of God that takest away the sins of the world,
have mercy upon us.
Lamb of God that takest away the sins of the world,
have mercy upon us.
Lamb of God that takest away the sins of the world,
grant us thy peace.

Communion

Take eat.

This is our Lord Jesus coming to us in bread. This is God's gift to us, his people.

(The bread is shared)

This is our Lord Jesus coming to us in wine. This is God's gift to us, his people.

(The wine is shared)

The peace of the Lord Jesus Christ be with you.

Prayers

Let us pray:

Loving Father, we thank you for your goodness to us at our Lord's table. As you have fed us with the bread and wine you have assured us of your everlasting love in Jesus your Son. We thank you for those who have gone before us in faith and are alive for ever in Christ Jesus. Help us to keep as close to Jesus each day of our lives as we have been in these moments of communion with him, and bring us at last with all your people to eat and drink with him in the glory of your eternal kingdom.

We pray for our congregation and for the church of Jesus Christ all over the world (pause)

We pray for those who are closest to us - family, relatives, friends, *and for those who care for us* (pause)

We pray for those we know who are sad or lonely or in trouble (pause)

We pray for........... *(person communicating)*
for .... (elder)
for .... (pastoral assistant/probationer/other person present)
and for .... (minister) (pause)

We pray for our world, for peace and justice and freedom (pause)

We pray that we may be inspired by your presence, steeped in your goodness, and directed by your wisdom, today and always, through Jesus Christ our Lord, Amen.

Blessing

The blessing of God, Father, Son and Holy Spirit, be upon you and remain with you always, Amen.

Notes

1 The versions of the Sanctus, Lord's Prayer and Agnus Dei quoted are taken from the 1940 version of the Book of Common Order.

2 Where words are in italics or there are dotted lines insertions should be made or words ommitted as appropriate.

3 Suitable Bible readings might include :
    Psalm 23
    Psalm 100
    Isaiah 40 : 28 – 31
    Isaiah 53 : 1 – 6
    Isaiah 55 : 1 – 3, 6 – 9
    Matthew 11 : 28 – 30
    John 6 : 27 – 29, 35, 37
    John 15 : 9 – 14, 16 – 17

(You will also find the full script for this service on my website under "Ministrycraft" – www.johncnicol.com and you are welcome to download, print and use it.)

Acknowledgements with thanks

Scriptures and additional materials are from:

The Good News Bible © 1994 published by the Bible Societies/HarperCollins Publishers Ltd., *UK Good News Bible* © American Bible Society 1966, 1971, 1976, 1992. Used with permission.

The Holy Bible, New International Version, copyright 1973, 1978, 1984 by the International Bible Society. Used by permission of Hodder & Stoughton Publishers, a member of the Hachette Livre UK Group. All rights reserved. "NIV" is a trademark of the International Bible Society. UK trademark number 1448790.

Page 4   Part of the opening prayer from the "Order for the Celebration of the Sacrament of the Lord's Supper or Holy Communion" – Book of Common Order of the Church of Scotland 1940

Page 4   Part of the opening prayer from the "First Order for the Sacrament of the Lord's Supper or Holy Communion" – Book of Common Order of the Church of Scotland 1994.

Page 5   Prayer 32 "At the Lord's Supper" from Contemporary Prayers – The Collected Edition edited by Caryl Micklem SCM Press Ltd

Page 160   Blessing from "Still Waters, Deep Waters" by
            Rowland Croucher © John Mark Ministries,
            Melbourne Australia.

Page 164   Blessing from "Rivers in the Desert" by Rowland
            Croucher © John Mark Ministries, Melbourne
            Australia.

Page 164   Benedictions 1 and 15 from Book of Commmon
            Order of the Church of Scotland 1994.

Page 167   Extract from Christmas 1943 - "Letters and Papers
            from Prison" by Deitrich Bonhoeffer © SCM Press
            1953.

Lightning Source UK Ltd.
Milton Keynes UK
10 March 2010

151191UK00001B/45/P